MULTI-SENSORY
PRAYER

Over 60 innovative ready-to-use ideas

Sue Wallace

Thanks

There are many people that I would like to thank, whose ideas and inspiration have made this resource book possible. Firstly, thanks to God for getting the project off the ground in the first place; the Visions Community, for letting me take the time to do this; Nick Howe, Helen Begley, Phil Brown and members of Holy Trinity, Leeds, for showing us what was possible with creative prayer techniques; Andii Bowsher for showing us the physical version of the Lord's Prayer and the newsprint variation; Malcolm Wallace, my partner, for being a wonderful constructive critic; the IBVM for first introducing me to some of these techniques when I was at school; Andy Robinson for the walkabout idea; Sharon Stinson for starting us off reviewing our days; Anne Gray for the 'tree of life' idea and the dough recipe; other alternative service groups around the country, particularly TSS in Bristol, Grace in London, The Mass in Nottingham, NOC and the Iona community; Robert Warren for his insight in encouraging the alternative worship movement to get off the ground; Graham Cray, for helping Visions get started; the staff of St Michael-le-Belfrey for their help; Jonny Baker for his encouragement and help; Bishop Stephen for telling us about Orthodox ways of praying and also for using nails as a reminder; the staff of Chartres Cathedral for letting us walk their labyrinth. To lots of other people who I've forgotten – I apologise for not including you, but in a list like this I'm bound to forget someone important!

SUbtle products are youth publications of Scripture Union, 207-209 Queensway, Bletchley, MK2 2EB, England. www.scriptureunion.org.uk

ISBN 1 85999 465 2

Unless otherwise marked, Scripture quotations taken from the HOLY BIBLE NEW INTERNATIONAL VERSION. © 1973, 1978, 1984 by International Bible Society. Anglicisation copyright © 1979, 1984, 1989. Used by permission of Hodder & Stoughton Ltd.

Other Scripture quotations from Good News Bible published by Bible Society and HarperCollins Publishers Ltd, UK © American Bible Society 1966, 1971, 1976, 1992. Used with permission.

British Library Cataloguing-in-Publication Data
A catalogue record for this book is available from the British Library.
Cover design by Marketing FX
Internal design by Sue Jackson
Illustrations by Mike Kazybrid
Printed and bound in Malta by Interprint

Contents

Introduction

This is a collection of prayer rituals and meditations that we, at the Visions Community in York, have found helpful, particularly over the past couple of years. We started by recognising how pitifully bad we were, both at teaching and at praying, and wanted to find new ways of expressing ourselves in prayer. We looked through various traditions, and found our inspiration from sources as diverse as Anglican prayer groups, the Iona community, the Orthodox church, Catholic monastic orders, charismatic churches and many alternative worship groups. During our experiments we found that different types of prayer seemed to suit different personalities. One person, for example, may find a particular ritual deeply helpful, whereas another person may be unable to take part, either because at the present moment this might be too painful, or because for some other reason they may find it uncomfortable. For this reason we think that it is important to announce that people are free to 'opt out' or just watch if they wish.

We also found that being active in our services helped spiritual truths to sink in more easily than if they had been expressed in sermon form alone. As the old Chinese proverb says: 'I hear and I forget. I see and I remember. I do and I understand.' This collection will hopefully inspire you to try new ways of praying in your church community. We hope you find it helpful and that it becomes a springboard from which you can jump into creating your own new prayer ideas.

Sue Wallace

Preparing your building

Before you start to use any of these prayer ideas it is a good idea to prepare your space for prayer. Different people find different sorts of environments prayerful, so it will be impossible to please everyone, but do your best to make your congregation or prayer group comfortable. In the church services where we do these prayer activities, we like to sit on beanbags or the floor for many of them. You may have access to prayer stools or comfortable chairs, or you may wish to bring in some chairs, rugs or floor cushions. Remember though, that not everyone is able to sit on the floor, so leave some chairs for those who need them.

We also like to play gentle music as a background to our prayers. For us, the most helpful music is usually gentle, ambient, synthesizer music, but we have also found plainchant music to be helpful. Your congregation's tastes in music might well be different. You might decide to use instrumental or classical music, or some sort of worship song on tape.

We also like to make our building smell and look prayerful too. We light some incense or fragrant oil, to make the building smell nice, and we usually have gentle light levels, perhaps using candles. We often use slide projectors to show images that complement the prayer, but you might decide to use banners or icons. Rugs on the floor or swathes of material draped around walls can make a hall building less spartan. Or you may be lucky enough to have beautiful images already in your church building, in the stained glass or on the walls. Perhaps you might be able to draw attention to them in some way, by spotlighting them, or rearranging your seating. With stained glass, you can use spotlights outside the building to illuminate the glass at night.

Generally, the four questions you need to ask yourself are:

1 Does it *look* welcoming?
2 Does it *smell* nice?
3 Does it *feel* comfortable?
4 Do the *sounds* I can hear enhance or distract our prayers?

The choice of how to prepare your building is entirely up to you. But give it some forethought because a prayer experience can be so much deeper if the distractions of uncomfortable seats, harsh lighting or sudden noises from outside are removed.

Safety note
Please be extremely careful when using candles, incense and other flammable items. Always place them where they cannot set light to carpets, furnishings or clothing and have a bucket of sand or fire extinguisher handy.

 1 Preparing for worship

You may wish to begin your session of prayer with some sort of stilling prayer exercise. This helps us to focus on God and get rid of some of the distractions of the day. As the Psalm says, 'Be still and know that I am God.' (Psalm 46:10)

Some members of your congregation or group may never have encountered this form of prayer before and may be a little wary or suspicious. Remember to give them the option of not taking part if they feel uncomfortable, but it might also be a good idea to reassure them that they aren't going to do anything unbiblical or unchristian, and that this is purely a way of preparing ourselves so we can pray more effectively. A breathing prayer may also be used for this purpose, or a physical prayer such as **Open hands**.

Resources
No special resources are needed.

Method
This method is best used when you are about to embark on some sort of imaginative prayer or Bible meditation. Ask everyone to put themselves in a position in which they feel comfortable. Ask them to squeeze their toes up very tight, asking God to help them let go of distractions. Then ask them to relax, imagining everything that gets in the way of them concentrating on prayer leaving them in the same way as the tension.

Then ask everyone to squeeze their leg

muscles in the same way – really tight – then to relax. Follow this up through the body, going through the stomach, the hands, the arms, the face. Finally, you may wish to read a 'peaceful' Bible verse such as John 14:27: Jesus said, 'Peace I leave with you; my peace I give you. I do not give to you as the world gives. Do not let your hearts be troubled and do not be afraid.'

2 Breathing prayers

This method of prayer can be used at the beginning of any service, or even in your everyday life when you feel yourself starting to get angry or stressed. It is called a breathing prayer. Here we have given you a couple of variations on the basic breathing prayer, or you could write a variation of your own.

Resources
No special resources are needed.

Method
For both these variations, the basic idea is to sit in a comfortable position and focus on your breathing for a minute. Then as you breathe in, ask the Holy Spirit to fill you and imagine the 'breath of God' filling you as your own breath goes in. As you breathe out, ask God to take away the things that are distracting you from worship.

Remind everyone to do this at a breathing pace that is natural for them, so that they feel comfortable and don't get faint. Repeat this prayer as often as you wish, but do it at least a few times to allow its meaning to 'sink in'.

Breathe in: Come Holy Spirit
Breathe out: Distractions
Breathe in: Come Holy Spirit
Breathe out: Distractions

You might want to play a song whilst this is going on, with a 'Come Holy Spirit' theme to it (either on tape or a live instrumental version), but ask people not to sing as this gets in the way of the breathing prayer.

A variation on this breathing prayer is to breathe in asking God to give you different

fruits of the Spirit, and to breathe out the bad feelings that are the opposite of these fruits. You can use this like a sort of repentance prayer to say 'sorry' (eg for the times we hate) and to ask for God's love to replace it.

Breathe in: love
Breathe out: hate

Breathe in: joy
Breathe out: worries

Breathe in: peace
Breathe out: stress

Breathe in: patience
Breathe out: impatience

Breathe in: kindness
Breathe out: pettiness

Breathe in: goodness
Breathe out: anger

Breathe in: faithfulness
Breathe out: selfishness

Breathe in: gentleness
Breathe out: hardness

Breathe in: self-control
Breathe out: recklessness

As this list is rather long, you might decide just to pick a few of these fruits to pray about, using the breathing prayer. As before, you will probably want to repeat the prayer to help its meaning sink in.

3 Everybody at once

This is a well-known prayer method which is sometimes known as 'Korean prayer'. We felt that it would be useful to include it here, however, as we discovered a variation of this method which has been very useful for us. A common problem with this method of prayer, particularly in small churches, is that there aren't enough people to talk at once and therefore to disguise an individual voice. Consequently people feel bashful and don't want to pray out loud. Another common problem is that somebody has to start and end the prayer and it can be embarrassing to discover that you are the only one talking. We found that playing a cassette tape of lots of people talking at once can solve this problem. A

tape like this can be made by getting a group of people together, scripting some prayers and recording all the voices talking at once. Some voices may be reading Bible passages or pieces of liturgy. You may also want to borrow some other cassette players and play tapes of voices speaking on these as well, at the same time. The most important part of making this tape is not the actual words used, but the *amount* of voices (get as many voices as you can) and the *tones* of the voices speaking. Make sure there are some high-pitched voices and some low-pitched voices on the tape.

Resources
No specific resources are needed, but a cassette player and the tape mentioned above would be helpful. A gong or bell may also be useful.

Method
Explain that you are going to do 'everybody at once' style prayer. The congregation can pray whatever words they like, as loudly as they like. The idea is that everybody prays out loud at the same time and the sounds of the different voices all cover each other. Give some sort of signal for when the prayer is going to start and finish, and give some ideas as to the theme of the prayer. For example, if you are praying for items in the news you may wish to give different headlines: people recently bereaved, areas of conflict in the world, etc.

The signal for the start and finish may be your headlines (if you have a microphone and can be heard over the talking). Otherwise you may wish to use a gong or bell to signal the start and finish of the prayer. If you are using a tape, you need to begin to fade up the cassette just after you have announced your headlines. Then fade down the cassette when people are beginning to stop praying out loud.

ANY NUMBER

4 The Annunciation

Resources
No special resources are needed.

Method
Appoint a good reader or storyteller to read the following script, get comfortable and let your imagination take you on a prayerful journey.

The Annunciation script
One of the ways God speaks to us is through our imaginations. Imagination is often neglected in church, yet, like our other gifts and talents, it can be used by God. This is an imaginative meditation based on Scripture. The idea behind it is to take a Bible passage and place yourself in the position of one of the characters in the story.

The Annunciation is one of the more widely known Bible passages, and because of this it is easy to switch off when it is heard. In this case we decided to keep the situation and some of the original words of the angel, but to update the scene into our lives to see what happened.

Before we start you'll probably want to get yourself comfortable. Find a position in which you feel you can rest and let your imagination wander. Closing your eyes might help too.

It's four o'clock on a Saturday afternoon. You're sitting alone at home, having a drink and relaxing. The room is warm and peaceful – not much noise from outside, just the gentle tapping of rain on the window. Suddenly though, you hear a loud knock on the door. It's not an angry knock, but it's gently insistent all the same. You walk to the door and open it.

To your surprise, a man is standing there. You've never seen him before. At least you think he's a man. Somehow it's a little unclear. He is casually dressed, in jeans and a jumper. He has a ponytail and he is smiling at you. 'Hello'. He greets you by your first name as if you are an old friend. You are puzzled and a little suspicious at first. Then he says, in a gentle voice, 'Can I come in? I've been sent by God and I have a message for you. If you look at me closely you'll know me... I'm an angel.'

You look closely at the figure on the doorstep. Somehow what he says doesn't seem so strange. He looks just like an ordinary person – no wings, no robe or sword – but there is something about his eyes that gives the game away. There's a glow, like the light of

8

inspiration: like those eyes might have seen things a human never has – eyes full of love.

For some reason, and you're not really sure why, your heart starts beating faster, as if something really important is going to happen soon.

You show the strange man in. You sit in the chair, by your drink, and he sits opposite. 'I sang when Christ was born,' he says. 'There were many of us singing that night, a huge choir in fact. I sang, in a smaller way, when you were born too, and I sang on the day when you first started to love God. But today I haven't come to sing. Today I have come to talk.

'You have a gift, although sometimes you ignore this gift. I hear you saying, "I'm not very good really". Or, "It's only a little thing. Nothing of importance." But at least one person has mentioned this gift haven't they? Tell me about it. And be straight. No false modesty. No false pride. Tell me as it is. As it seems to you now.'

Now you tell the angel about your gift. (Pause for a minute or two.)

When you've finished telling the angel about your gift, you realize something. You suddenly remember the Jewish teenager who had an angel visit her. She had a talent for being a good mother – a talent she needed as her task was to care for a child who would have more questions, more pain and more confusion than any ordinary child. And much more to go through. You wonder if she knew she had this talent when the angel came? Or did it come as a complete surprise? (Short pause)

Then the angel looks at you once more and says, 'You are thought highly of by God. He loves you.' And then he calls you by name, by the name you call yourself in your head, and then he calls you talented, in the gift you told him about.

A thrill runs down your spine. A shiver of anticipation, and yet fear. The angel says, 'Don't be afraid, gifted one. God is pleased with you. He has a task he wishes you to do with the talent you have.'

And then you listen as the angel tells you of the task to be done. Listen to what he says. (Leave a long pause.)

After he has finished, you remember Mary once more. You remember how scared she must have been when the angel told her the task that she had to do: to give birth to the Son of God. You remember then the reply she gave to the angel: "I am the Lord's servant. May it happen to me just as you have said.'

And if you are ready (and only if you feel you can, because there is no point in lying to God) say your reply to the angel.

After you have said your reply, you get up from your chair. Suddenly you see the room is empty. The stranger has gone and you're not really sure whether he has used the door or not.

If you found this helpful you might want to write down what the angel said to you and put it somewhere to remind yourself later.

5 Incense I

This prayer ritual can be used in a variety of situations and with a variety of themes. It can be particularly good when interceding for friends who are ill or going through difficult times, and when all the information cannot be publicly broadcast. It is also good for people who are shy about praying in public.

Resources
You will need: a small barbecue (clean off all traces of fat beforehand); some charcoal (church charcoal should work fine); grains of solid church incense (this is available from an ecclesiastical bookshop as is the charcoal): a thurible (see below); pencils and pieces of writing paper: a large candle: a large, or well-ventilated venue (this can get a bit smoky!)

Method
About five minutes before this ritual is due to start, light the charcoal and give it time to start

to glow red. If you wish to speed this process up, using a thurible (censer) will help get air to the charcoal. (See instructions in **Incense II** on how to make a thurible if your church hasn't got one.)

When you are ready to begin the intercession, light the candle and place it beside a bowlful of incense grains near the barbecue. Give the pieces of paper and the pencils out and explain that the idea is to write our intercessory prayers down on the pieces of paper. When all these have been written, allow people to go up, in their own time, wrap some incense grains in the paper, light the paper from the candle and place in the barbecue. You may wish to read a passage of Scripture such as Psalm 141 or Revelation 8:3,4 (below):

'Another angel, who had a golden censer, came and stood at the altar. He was given much incense to offer, with the prayers of all the saints, on the golden altar before the throne. The smoke of the incense, together with the prayers of the saints, went up before God from the angel's hand. Then the angel took the censer, filled it with fire from the altar, and hurled it on the earth; and there came peals of thunder, rumblings, flashes of lightning and an earthquake.'

Give plenty of time for people to write their prayers on the pieces of paper. You will probably find that some people wish to write far more than others. As people burn their prayers on the barbecue, the grains of incense melt and the smoke rises towards the ceiling. Watching this can be very moving.

 **6 Incense II**   ANY NUMBER

This is a method of prayer using incense as a blessing. You may wish to do this as a preparation prayer, incensing different parts of your building and praying for God to come and fill it with his presence.

Resources
You will need: church charcoal; church incense (available from an ecclesiastical bookshop); a thurible (censer). (These can be extremely expensive to buy if you don't have one, so see below for instructions on how to make one of your own.)

How to make a thurible (or censer)
You will need: a tin can (a can that is wider than average seems to work best); some metal wire or chain; a bradawl or a screwdriver, and a hammer.

Take the tin can (we used an old sweetcorn tin), remove the label and punch lots of small holes in the sides (with the screwdriver or bradawl) at regular intervals. Make sure there are plenty of holes as near to the bottom of the can as possible. This will allow the maximum airflow to the charcoal. Then punch three large holes near the top of the tin to attach the chain or wire to. This will become your handle. You can find a variety of different types of cheap chain at most DIY stores. Any of these will do. When we first made our thurible we used string for the handle, but this has the disadvantage of being damaged or burned very easily, so it is not very safe. Once the handle is attached, your censer is ready for use.

Method
Light a couple of pieces of charcoal (this is most easily done with a candle) and place in your thurible. Be careful, as when the charcoal is newly lit it tends to spit sparks, so place in the thurible as quickly as possible. Then swing or spin the thurible quickly to get as much air as you can to the charcoal. (If you don't get enough air to it quickly enough it will go out.) After a little while, the coal will begin to glow red. When it has reached this stage, place a pile of incense into the middle of each charcoal round with a teaspoon, and you are ready to go.

It's up to you what happens next. You may want to light the incense at the beginning of the service and bless each member of the congregation with it as they enter the church, or just before you start the service. (Perhaps use appropriate words such as 'welcome', 'God be with you', or an original phrase appropriate to each person's talents.)

Alternatively, you could pray around the building with the incense. Visit all the places where things happen such as the pulpit, the lectern, the Communion table, the choir stalls, the organ, the piano. You may just pray a simple prayer either out loud or quietly, such as 'Come Holy Spirit and be with (for example) our singing', or you may wish to pray a Celtic-style blessing (such as the one below) as you move around.

*May God give his blessing to the house that is
   here.
And bless this place from roof... to floor,
from wall... to wall...,
from end... to end...,
From the deepest foundation...
To the highest tower.*

*In the strong name of the Trinity,
Banish all evil,
Cease all fighting.
Christ's Spirit alone
Dwell within these walls.*

UP TO 60 /ADAPTABLE

7 Christ the Healer

This ritual was written for a service about Christ the Healer. We found this service particularly difficult to plan, due to the fact that our parent church has been particularly good at teaching about healing prayer and making this available after every service. We therefore looked for a different 'angle' we could use for the service. This we found in the story of Naaman the leper.

Resources
You will need: seven large bowls full of warm water and containing some form of (preferably hypo-allergenic) bubble bath; seven towels; large labels to place by each bowl.

Method
Read the story of Naaman the leper in 2 Kings 5:1–15. Then give this introduction:

Naaman was asked to wash seven times in the Jordan river. So here we have seven bowls for washing in. Each of these bowls are symbolic of something that stands in the way

of us being externally healed, or internally or spiritually whole. All of us are different. We each have our own problems and difficulties, and our own doubts and fears. If you find you wish to wash in one bowl but you find you cannot honestly wash in another then please feel free to do this.
Now I'll briefly explain the names on the bowls and what they might mean:
1 Guilt – This bowl is a chance for us to apologise to God for anything that we feel we have done wrong this week. It's also a chance to ask God to free us from any guilt feelings that are clinging to us. Sometimes we know in our heads that Christ has forgiven us for something we did wrong, yet we still feel very guilty, and perhaps find it hard to forgive ourselves.
2 Grudges – Sometimes we find it hard to forgive someone else for hurting us in some way. And somewhere at the back of our minds it nags at us, getting in the way of our growth. This is what this bowl is about – asking God to help us forgive, to take away the pain, and to give us a willingness to love once more.
3 Expectations – There are so many ways in which our expectations can get in the way of us being healed. In the story, Naaman expected to be healed of his leprosy by the prophet speaking grand words over him. He didn't expect to have to wash in a muddy river. Sometimes we expect God to work in a certain way: in church, not outside; using a vicar, not an ordinary person; using a set form of words or actions, not an informal prayer.
4 Prejudices – Naaman's prejudices about washing in a Jewish river almost stopped him being healed. We all have different prejudices. Perhaps this is a prejudice against a different type of church or a method of worship. Or perhaps it is a prejudice about a person.
5 Impatience – Sometimes we are ill, hurting inside, or just confused for a very long time. And the fact that we aren't healed straightaway makes us think it'll never happen. We live in an instant society that drinks instant coffee, watches instant entertainment on the TV, and expects instant results from healing prayer. Or we give up.
6 Cynicism – It's easy to get cynical sometimes when Christians say cruel or thoughtless things to hurting people. Or

maybe there are other things around us, like friends losing their faith or having painful experiences that make us feel cynical.

7 Pride – Sometimes we are too proud to even ask for help. We like people to think we can stand on our own two feet. Or maybe we find it difficult to ask for things because we are shy or are scared of being rejected.

Now we're going to have a time when we sit and pray silently. If and when you feel ready, do feel free to come and prayerfully wash in any or all of the bowls.

UP TO 60/ADAPTABLE

8   The tree of life

This is more of a Bible-based meditation, linking our experiences of healing plants with the tree of life in the book of Revelation.

Resources
You will need: leaves from a tree (a medicinal tree or bush such as eucalyptus or mint would be best for this).

Method
Give out the leaves, one to each person. Then appoint a good reader to read the following script.

The tree of life script
Look at your leaf closely. See the colours within it, the veins and the stalk. (Pause) Marvel at its intricacy. (Pause)

Thank God for paying so much loving attention to something so small and delicate. Remember that God pays even more attention to you, you who are worth more than many leaves, trees or birds that sit in them.

Scratch your leaf or break it in half. Smell it. Notice its ability to help you breathe more easily – its ability to make your nostrils tingle a little. (Short pause)

The book of Revelation says this: 'The angel also showed me the river of the water of life, sparkling like crystal, and coming from the throne of God and of the Lamb, and flowing down the middle of the

city's street. On each side of the river was the tree of life, which bears fruit twelve times a year, once each month; and its leaves are for the healing of the nations' (Revelation 22:1,2 GNB).

In the past we understood about trees being for healing. We used willow bark as aspirin for our headaches, mint for our digestion and eucalyptus for our colds. We understood that these plants were precious gifts of God for us. Think about some of these plants and herbs now, and spend some time thanking God for the healing leaves he has given us. (Pause) Sometimes these days we forget how fragile and dependent we are on God's gifts. We get our medicines from tablets in childproof bottles, divorced from the healing plants in the field. Yet we are still dependent on them as scientists scour the remaining rainforest for new medicinal plants, hoping to find a cure for cancer, for Parkinson's disease, for AIDS. Let's spend some time now praying for those whose diseases seem incurable. (Pause)

The leaves of the tree are for the healing of the nations.

Finally, let's think of the tree of life in Revelation. Let's thank God for the hope that one day we will all be truly well and whole. Not only healed of the pains and diseases we suffer now, but also cured of the prejudices, hate, pride and selfishness that hurt other people so much.

UP TO 60/ADAPTABLE

9   Broken dreams

This prayer ritual was originally produced for a service based on the parable of the ten virgins. We talked about how, for some people, the lamp of hope had gone out and why that might be so. We talked about shattered hopes and broken dreams. This ritual is a way of expressing those broken dreams and disappointments before God, and asking God to make them into something new.

Resources
You will need: broken pieces of pottery or tiles (bathroom or kitchen tiles work particularly

well); tile grout and tile adhesive; a simple wooden cross (two pieces of wood nailed together is fine); pencils.

Method

Ask people to write their broken dreams and disappointments onto the back of these broken pieces of pottery. Give them time to think about these things, and to have a chance to pray that God would make something new out of them. Then, when everyone is ready, spread tile adhesive over the cross, and let everyone place their broken piece of pottery (writing side down) where they wish to upon the cross. When everyone has finished, allow the group to fill in any spaces in the tiles as they wish, allow the tile adhesive to dry, and grout the whole thing together (and varnish afterwards if you wish). Colour may be added to the grout if you want. When the mosaic cross is finished use it as part of a Communion service at a later date.

`ANY NUMBER`

 10 Ash Wednesday

This is a variation on an old theme, connecting Ash Wednesday with getting rid of the fake idols, temptations or concerns in our lives.

Resources

You will need: a large flameproof bowl (metal works best) or barbecue; a lit candle to light the objects with; a collection of 'idols' eg advertisements from magazines, bread, a cheque for a million pounds, fashion magazines and a piece of cloth (cotton), pictures of film stars, a stick, a beer mat, a flower.

Half a firelighter will be useful to help things get going. (Have a bucket of sand or a fire extinguisher nearby just in case things get out of hand!) You can make your own variations on these things by substituting objects that have meaning for you and your group. (For example, in a younger group you may wish to substitute a paper cup from a burger bar for the beermat). Try and choose things to burn that will not give off toxic fumes (ie no plastics or synthetic fibres).

Method

This works best when a different person comes up to the brazier to place each object into it, burn it and pray an appropriate prayer. As each person goes up, ask them to announce what the object is, in case people at the back of the church cannot see easily.

1st person (a collection of adverts)
Father, we are always running after things. We want bigger, better things, listening too hard to the adverts of our consumer society. Protect us from this greed. Help us to cling to the important things instead: compassion, love, hope and joy, the treasures of heaven.

2nd person (pictures of famous people)
Father, help us to turn away from our lust for fame – when we secretly want people to recognise our achievements and congratulate us over them. Give us reassurance when we are doing the right thing, and the energy to work at spreading your fame instead of our own.

3rd person (a stick)
Father, help us to turn away from our thirst for power – when we accidentally or deliberately manipulate others, beating them down with the stick of our power or ambitions. Forgive us when we use your Holy Book as an excuse to injure others or as a cover for our pride.

4th person (a cheque)
Father, help us to conquer our desire for money. Help us to see money in perspective, as a tool to help others instead of a weapon against the poor.

5th person (a slice of bread)
Father, we sometimes get so obsessed by food – whether it be by eating too much, by dieting, or by worrying about what foods are safe to eat. Help us to eat joyfully, safely and without greed. Help us also to do our part to help the hungry.

6th person (fashion magazines and a piece of cloth)
Father, help us not to follow fashion blindly, but to appreciate the beauty and creativity of clothing as art whilst making sure no one is hurt by fashion – either by being forced to buy expensive clothes by peer pressure, or by

being forced to work in a clothing factory for a slave wage.

7th person (a beer mat)
Father, sometimes we can get so hedonistic – just wanting the next 'high' whether it be from drink, drugs or religious experiences. Help us to enjoy the times of happiness you give us, but not to pursue it by hurting other people or our own bodies.

8th person (a flower)
Father, help us to turn away from our misuse of beauty. Help us not to view people as sex objects rather than human beings with feelings that can be hurt. Help us not to judge people by their outward looks, but to look for everyone's inner beauty.

When the ash is cool enough to be safe, put a spot of the ash on the forehead of everyone who wants to join in. You may need to sing a song or do some other event whilst the ash is cooling.

You may wish to say something when you place the ash on everyone's forehead – perhaps something like, 'Remember you'd be dust without God who gives you life.'

You may wish to finish with a communal prayer something like this:
We resolve to use clothing for good, to bring colour to dark corners and warmth to those suffering from cold, to give God the fame, to bring power to the powerless, to use money as an ally to help the poor. We resolve to feed the hungry and make sure food producers are paid fair wages, to bring joy and happiness to the sad and lonely, to look for the true beauty in human souls and to foster it. We resolve to chase after lasting treasure rather than the treasure that turns to ashes.

UP TO 60

11 Walkabout
(from an idea by Andy Robinson)

This is a more physical method of prayer, involving going on a prayerful walk around the inside or the outside of a building.

Resources
No specific resources are needed unless you wish to place pictures, posters or newspaper cuttings around the building to aid people's prayers. A gong or bell may also be useful to signal the end of the walk.

Method
Explain that you are going to go on a prayer walk, and give a rough idea of how long the walk is going to last (eg five minutes). Explain what a prayer 'walkabout' actually is.

Example walkabout script
We are going to take time now for five minutes or so to go on a prayer 'walkabout' around or outside the building. You can go anywhere you like, in any order, but don't go too far out of earshot. The idea behind this is that as we walk we observe many things we might otherwise not notice – the office block across the road from the church, the poster for the local homeless shelter – and we can pray about these things. I will ring a bell at the end of this time and then we shall gather back here once more.

This 'walkabout' method can also be extended in time and distance to perhaps walking entirely around a local block of streets in the parish, quietly praying for the residents or anything else you may see on your journey.

UP TO 60/ADAPTABLE

12 The hazelnut

This meditation was originally written for an alternative worship gathering in York. It would especially suit a service with a creation theme. It is based on recent scientific discoveries combined with the words of Julian of Norwich.

Resources
You will need: a bag of hazelnuts in their shells. (Make sure that no one participating has an allergy to nuts. Even the oil from nuts can cause skin rashes if you're allergic to them.)

Method
Start the meditation by handing around the hazelnuts to everyone. Ask them to hold them in the palms of their hands and look at them for a little while.

Hazelnut script

Voice 1: This meditation is in two sections. The first is taken from science. The second is by Julian of Norwich. You may wish to close your eyes for this part of the meditation. But keep the hazelnut in your hand.

Voice 2: If we look into the sky on a clear night we can see an amazing shimmering carpet of stars, each a gleaming point of light, shining like a diamond. If the visibility is good we can count them, and, if we don't lose count, we might be able to see as many as three thousand stars. Scientists tell us that each of these stars is really a huge ball of burning fire, like our own sun or even bigger, sometimes shining more brightly, sometimes darker and dimmer. Yet this shining carpet is only the tip of the cosmic iceberg. As time has passed, we have built ever larger telescopes and seen further and further away. We now know that the shining carpet of stars we can see with the naked eye is just the nearest corner of our universe.

We live on a small planet orbiting a medium-sized star called the sun, which is on the outskirts of a spiral galaxy called the Milky Way. This contains 100,000 million stars which, if they were grains of sand, would be enough sand to fill a small room. Yet many scientists believe there are 100,000 million other galaxies. Imagine how many rooms, streets and towns they would fill if each star was a grain of sand. These are so far away that they are impossible to comprehend using ordinary means. So instead, scientists have developed measurements using light. The distance travelled by light in an empty space in a year is called a light year. This is about six million, million miles. Yet light takes around four years to travel from Alpha Centauri, which is the nearest star to us outside our solar system. And light takes a mind-boggling two million light years to get from the nearest galaxy, Andromeda, to us. That is the furthest we can see with the naked eye. Using telescopes though, the furthest we can see is around a hundred thousand billion, billion miles and increasing all the time. Yet, even with the advent of the Hubble space telescope, we still cannot see anywhere near the end of the created universe, and the distances involved are too huge for our brains to even properly imagine.

Voice 1: He also showed me a little thing, about the size of a hazelnut, in the palm of my hand; and it was as round as a ball. I looked at it, trying to understand it, and thought "What might this be?" And I was answered like this: "It is everything that has been made". I was amazed that it could last, for I thought it might suddenly have collapsed into nothing, it was so little. And a voice spoke inside my thoughts: "It lasts, and ever shall last because God loves it. And so everything exists because of the love of God.

So in this Little Thing I saw three lessons.
The first is that God made it,
the second is that God loves it,
and the third is that it is God who keeps it going.

(Author's translation based on *Revelations of Divine Love* by Julian of Norwich, Christian Classics Etherial Library. Copyright 1999.)

UP TO 60/ADAPTABLE

13 Graffiti

This prayer technique is good for public intercession: perhaps praying for areas of conflict in the world, or praying for our country. It helps if the subject of the 'prayer graffiti' is made fairly specific so that people know what to write about. If you are about to have a room in your church or church hall redecorated you may decide to graffiti the walls of this room with prayer before you redecorate.

Resources

You will need: a wall or noticeboard covered in a large piece of paper (you could put brick patterns on this paper to make it seem more like a graffiti wall); lots of paint or marker pens (of differing colours). If paint is used, brushes will also be needed, and plastic sheets or newspaper to cover the floor will also be helpful.

Method

Explain the subject of the graffiti wall (such as war zones) and then invite people to come up to the wall, in their own time, and write or paint whatever slogans and prayers they wish on the wall. They may also draw pictures if they feel easier expressing their prayers in this way. At the end of the prayer session you may wish to summarise these prayers in some way, perhaps by writing 'Lord, hear our prayers' or something similar at the bottom of the wall.

14 Money

At other times in our worship services we have talked about giving or about ethical banking. One time we decided to use a meditation as a means of thinking about money; what it is really like, why we use it and to pray for those who are hurt by its misuse. This meditation is not intended to replace teaching on giving or banking, but rather to complement it.

Resources
You will need: a collection of money in coins or notes. Preferably use some foreign or historical ones such as Roman coins if you can get some. Perhaps include some foreign notes of high denominations. This helps us to realise that we attach value to something that is really quite valueless.

Method
Before you start, let the congregation pick up a coin or note of their choice. Appoint a good reader to read the following script.

Money script
Let's start by getting relaxed. Shuffle about until you're in a position where you really feel comfortable. Then close your eyes for a moment and we'll start with a breathing prayer. As you breathe in, ask God to come and speak to you. As you breathe out, let go of anything that is standing in your way, such as any distractions. Do this a few times at your own pace. (Pause for a while.)

Now open your eyes and look at your coin or note. Imagine you've never seen a coin before. Look at its colours and the patterns upon it, touch it, feel its texture. In itself it has very little value. In itself it's neither good nor bad. Its value is the value we give to it, which may be very great, or may be very small. What things does it represent? Food, warmth,

clothing? (Short pause)
Some people can only afford these.
To others it represents the good things in life. The luxuries. (Short pause)
None of these coins are new. Some are very old.
What story might your coin have to tell if it could talk?
How many hands has it passed through before coming here? (Pause)
It may have travelled a long way, from another country. It may have been wept over or kept in the purse of someone who had very little, and worried over. How to pay all these bills? The little coins become all the more important when there are hardly any of them. (Short pause)
It may have been kept in the purse of someone who could spare little and yet given away. Freely. In love. Knowing there were no others left. But God was watching. Christ said, 'I tell you truly, this poor widow has put more into the treasury than all the others. They all gave out of their wealth; but she, out of her poverty, put in everything – all she had to live on.' (Short pause)

It's only a small coin. It's probably never done a great deal of harm in its time. But what about its big brothers – the cheques and the plastic money? They have been used to harm sometimes: kept in the hands of a weapons dealer, a torturer, a loan shark with no compassion... Think now of the victims of these people. Pray for them. (Longer pause)

Remember that Jesus too was betrayed for money. Thirty pieces of silver: the price of a slave; the price on the head of the Son of God. He too knew what it was like to be hurt by another's greed.

When you have finished, if you want to, you could bring the coin or note to the altar, as a sign of giving yourself and your money worries to God.

As some offering prayers remind us, when we give God money we are only giving him back what belongs to him.

15 Newsprint

This method of intercessory prayer can be used as part of a service on almost any theme. It works particularly well if the finished article is taken in procession to the Communion table and used as a cloth during the liturgy. Or you could cut the cloth or card into the shape of a pair of hands as a sign that you wish to place these problems in God's hands.

Resources
You will need: a selection of newspapers (preferably no more than a week old); lots of scissors; glue (PVA glue works best); a large piece of paper, cardboard or white cloth.

Method
Give a newspaper (or a section of a newspaper) and some scissors to everyone in the congregation. Ask them to prayerfully look through the headlines and pick out anything that strikes them as being important to pray about. Cut these articles out. Place the large piece of paper or card at the front of the church. Place some pots of glue around this area and perhaps cushions to kneel on. Invite the congregation to come up, kneel down, and stick the news articles upon the card or paper. You may wish to have some sort of action to summarise these prayers, such as a verbal prayer summing up the articles being prayed for, or a section later in the service when the congregation can view the finished collage and say their 'Amen' to other's prayers in some way, eg by lighting candles around the collage, or by walking past the finished collage.

Variations
As a variation on this, you may decide to actually write prayers onto the newspaper articles themselves before sticking them onto the card. In this case you will need to have plenty of pens available.

16 North, South, East, West

This is a method of intercession that can work very well in a variety of different church situations. It is a good way of introducing physical movement into a church service where the church building doesn't allow much room for the congregation to physically walk around.

Resources
You will need: signs or posters with names of different countries or areas of a town on them. Projections of maps or place names can also be used. A compass and an atlas or town map may also be useful.

Method
Many old churches are built with the Communion table at the east end. If you do not know which direction your church faces, look it up on a map or use a compass and find out which direction different countries are in relation to your building. Instead of using different countries you may wish to pray for different streets, suburbs or areas of the town around your church. Place signs or posters of the names of these places around your building, as accurately as you can in relation to your atlas or map.

Ask the congregation to stand and face north. If they wish they may want to stretch their hands out towards the different places in that direction. Then have a time when people can pray for these countries or places. Decide which method of doing this might be the best for your church situation and give instructions accordingly. The congregation may wish just to say the names of the places on the signs out loud, or they may wish to pray silently. They may wish to pray longer prayers out loud in turn, or 'everybody at once' style. Then ask everybody to turn and face east. Repeat this procedure for all the four points of the compass. You could also vary this prayer technique by using picture slides showing places or countries in the different directions.

17   Using candles – I

There are many different ways in which candles can be used in prayer. This is just one of them. Many people take comfort from lighting a candle for someone they know is suffering and this, particularly, is the idea that this ritual is based on.

Resources:
You will need: candles; small plastic boxes full of wet sand (seed trays are quite good for this); a collection of broken things (broken glasses, pieces of pottery, old radios or televisions, pictures that are ripped, etc). It is best if it is obvious that the things are broken.

Method
Take the collection of broken things and form into some sort of sculpture, perhaps arranging them so that they form a tower, mountain or even a cross. Explain that we are going to spend some time thinking of people who feel that they are broken or suffering in some way. Play a piece of instrumental music and give people time to think about the people they know who might be feeling like this. Give out some candles and ask the congregation to light a candle as they pray for the person they've been thinking about. Place the boxes of sand near to the sculpture and use the sand as a base to stand the lit candles in.

18   Using candles – II

This prayer method works particularly well at Easter time when you can use the large Paschal (Easter) candle to pass around.

Resources
You will need: a large candle (make sure that the candle is wide enough so that the wax doesn't drip over the church or over the congregation).

Method
Announce that you are going to pass the candle around the church, and as it reaches each person ask them to say the name of someone they wish to pray for out loud (just the first name is fine or they can say both names if they wish). You might wish to explain that the candle is a symbol of the light of Christ, and we would like to pray that Christ would touch the people we name with his light and love. If you are using a Paschal candle, you might also wish to explain that the Chi-Rho (XP) sign on the side is Christ's initials in Greek. You may find it helpful to dim the lights a little so that people can see the candlelight moving around the church, and you may wish to play or sing some sort of appropriate song during this prayer time. Perhaps sing a song about the light of Christ, or maybe a song about prayer, such as 'Lord hear my prayer' from the Taizé Community. At the end of the prayer time bring the candle to the front of the church. You may like to keep it alight for the rest of the service.

A variation on this idea is to place some barbed wire around the top of the candle (as in the *Amnesty International* symbol) and, as the candle is passed around, to pray for areas of the world where Christians are being persecuted (see **Prisoners**, p53). Make sure that the barbed wire is well away from where people's hands will hold the candle.

19   Advent (bricks)

This prayer ritual works particularly well when used as part of a Communion service during Advent. The aim of the ritual is to construct a table or an altar out of the bricks and perspex, which will then be used for the Communion liturgy later in the service.

Resources
You will need: a collection of bricks (although these can be expensive, some builders will let you borrow some bricks for this purpose which can be returned later); a table top (a sheet of perspex or safety glass works well for this).

Method

Have piles of bricks scattered around the church near members of the congregation. You may find it helpful to sing or play the tune 'Prepare ye the way of the Lord' from the musical *Godspell*, or you may use a poem or quote from a film about building to help you. We found a quote from the film *Field of Dreams* which said 'If you build it he will come' very helpful.

There are a number of Bible passages that you may wish to use as inspiration. Invite the congregation each to bring a brick, come up to the front of the church and place their brick onto the others to build up the legs of a Communion table, as a sign that they offer themselves to help build God's kingdom on earth.

It is probably a good idea to put markings on the floor where the bricks need to go to make a table (or you can place some bricks in place already as a base). You may wish to be on hand to advise anyone who is not sure where to put their brick. When everybody has placed a brick in place, put the table top onto them and continue with the Communion liturgy.

20 Pray-dough

Resources

You will need: a large lump of dough, modelling material or clay. (See recipe for how to make some dough for yourself. If real clay is to be used make sure it has been thoroughly 'worked' first to remove excess water.) You will also need bowls and towels for washing with afterwards.

Method

The first time this method of prayer is used it can be quite daunting. Explain that it doesn't matter what the finished article looks like, it can be quite abstract. What is important is our feelings as we work the clay or dough. These are our prayerful expressions to God. Sometimes people find it helpful to work the clay in the dark, which makes them less self-

conscious about their artistic abilities. The first time this is used as a method of prayer it is best to confine it to a specific theme that is not too inward-looking, such as intercession for areas of conflict in the world. On later occasions it may be appropriate to focus more inwardly, or on difficult themes, but it is wise to bear in mind that this may bring up painful memories for some people and that they may need prayer or counselling afterwards.

Give a lump of clay or dough to each person, and a tray or plate of some sort for them to lean on. Then give plenty of time for people to express themselves in prayer using the clay. At the end of this period of prayer, you may wish to have a procession of some sort when the trays are taken to the foot of the cross, or placed near the Communion table. Why not finish with some sort of hand-washing ritual, so that people can serve each other by washing one another's hands as they will probably be a little dirty?

Recipe for Pray-dough

Ingredients: 2 cups flour; 1 cup salt; 2 tbsp oil; 2 cups water; 2 tsp cream of tartar (this is very important); a few drops of food colouring.

Method

Put all your ingredients into a pan and mix together. Heat gently, stirring continually until the mixture gradually starts to go gooey. When the mixture comes away from the sides of the pan it is ready to use. (If you heat the mixture too long it will be too hard to work easily. If you don't heat the mixture long enough it will be too gooey to use easily). When you have finished heating your mixture, knead it well, allow to cool and it will be ready to use.

21 The globe

This is another method of praying for the world and gives members of the congregation a chance to intercede for countries that they are particularly concerned about, or countries that are not often mentioned in public prayers.

Resources
You will need: a large globe of some description (plastic inflatable ones work well).

Method
Pass the globe around the room or church from person to person. Encourage people to call out the name of a country as they hold the globe. They may pray a longer prayer than this if they wish, but it isn't necessary. The globe may be passed around more than once, and more than one globe may be passed around the building at the same time (as many as you wish). This may be particularly important if there are a lot of people in your congregation. When you have finished, you may like to place the globes at the front of the church somewhere, for example, at the foot of the cross or on the Communion table.

22 Blessings

We have used this type of blessing ourselves and also seen it used effectively in other churches. It can make you feel very special as you are blessed 'personally' rather than as part of a large group.

Resources
You will need: flower petals, or confetti or glitter; a spotlight (if glitter is to be used).

Method
Encourage the group or congregation to leave the worship space one or two at a time. Have two people standing at a point along the way (for example an archway, the end of the pews or a doorway). Stand these people on stools or pews to raise them above the heads of the

other worshippers. As the congregation passes, throw some flower petals (or another substitute) over their heads and say a short blessing such as, 'You are special and loved by God' or 'The Lord bless you and keep you'. The church minister can say this blessing from beside the petal throwers, or even be one of these people. You could vary the blessing used for each two people to make it seem more personal. If glitter is used for the blessing, point a spotlight (or two) at the place where the glitter falls to make it shimmer in the light.

A variation on this blessing is that you can have the congregation remaining in their places and walk around 'blessing' them where they sit. This may be more appropriate in churches with no obvious 'aisle', with the elderly or disabled, or when you wish the worshippers to remain in the worship space for some reason.

Another variation is that you can gather the congregation outside the worship space before an event and have the 'blessing' as a sort of welcome: 'You are special and loved by God. We welcome you.' Or you may give the flower petals to the congregation during a baptism or confirmation service, and have the congregation welcoming the 'newcomers' by showering them with flowers.

23 Seeds of hope

Variations on this prayer ritual are quite good to do during Lent or for services on suffering, death, powerlessness or lack of hope. On different occasions you can use the seeds as symbols of different things. This is just one of those themes.

Resources
You will need: a large bowl or tub; a big bag of earth; bulbs or seeds that are in season. (Seeds large enough to hold without getting lost are best. Ask advice from your local garden centre.)

Method
Fill the large bowl full of earth and place it at

the front of the church. Give one seed or bulb to each person in the congregation and let them hold them. Then find a reader to read the script. After the seeds have been planted, place them in a prominent place, perhaps beside the entrance to the church, so that the congregation can watch them grow and flower.

Seeds of hope script

You have in your hand a seed. Small and delicate, who would think that such amazing new life could come out of something so small and brittle? But for that life to come it must go into the cold dark earth. Sometimes we feel that all around us life is dark, or maybe we know someone who is feeling like that now. There seems to be no sun, no warmth. Life seems like one, long, cold winter. Perhaps you are afraid for the future. Will spring ever come, or will the seeds of my faith die in the cold, dark earth?

Now take a moment to ask God to shine his light into the darkness of your fears and pain. Ask God to warm the cold earth of your life with his love, and imagine that seed growing for a moment. (Short pause) New life coming out of our dead, cold world – the life of resurrection. Growing ever taller, to become a thing to give joy and beauty to many people. Jesus said, 'Unless a grain of wheat falls to the ground and dies, it remains only a single seed.' He also said, 'I am the resurrection and the life.'

Now, when you are ready, and if you feel you can, plant your seed. And as you plant it, pray that the light of hope and resurrection will come to the dark situations in our lives.

UP TO 60

24 Offerings

There are many variations on this offering prayer and it is particularly appropriate when used in a Communion service. You may wish to give the congregation some notice the week before so that they remember to bring something from their daily work to church. Or you may decide to do something more personal and let the congregation bring out

something that they are wearing on their person: a piece of jewellery, a diary or some keys. Of course, there has to be a certain amount of trust in the congregation (eg that no-one will run away with your car keys!) to do this. Another variation on this is to use this as a morning daily prayer, and to give items to God that are in some way symbolic of the things you are going to do that day.

Resources

You will need: an altar or Communion table or a large cross; an advance notice if you wish the congregation to bring something special.

Method

Announce that you are going to have a special offering time when people can come up and place something symbolic of themselves or their jobs upon the table, altar or cross. Allow plenty of time for people to come up and place items on the table. Then, if it is a Communion service, finally bring out the bread and wine. When Communion is served, the congregation can take back again the things they brought to the front. This is symbolic of the fact that we give our lives to God but that he gives us back eternal lives, transformed and made whole. If you are not having a Communion service you may wish to use a cross instead of a table and to express God giving us our life back in some other way, perhaps by giving everyone a flower as they take their items back.

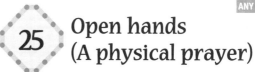

ANY NUMBER

25 Open hands (A physical prayer)

Some people may find physical praying uncomfortable, or be mistrustful of a method of prayer they are unfamiliar with. Some of these prayers may remind them of the 'action songs' they used to do as a child and this may put them off. Yet 'Body prayer' can be a very powerful thing; expressing truths that are difficult to put into words or allowing our bodies to worship God. As the Bible says: 'Love the Lord your God with all your heart and with all your soul and with all your strenght' (Deuteronomy 6:5) and 'offer your

bodies as living sacrifices' (Romans 12:1). This prayer is a way of worshipping God with our strength and reminding us to offer our bodies to God in our daily lives.

Resources

No special physical resources are needed but you need to bear in mind that, in order to teach these prayers in a church, you will either need some sort of hands-free radio microphone that will not get tangled up when you are moving, or a couple of people at the front of the church to demonstrate the prayer actions whilst you explain what they mean.

Method

We have found this prayer to be good as a preparation prayer before a worship session. It also has the advantage that it can be done sitting, standing or kneeling down.

First get into a comfortable position to pray. Decide whether to do the prayer sitting, standing or kneeling. It doesn't really matter which of these positions are used, but changing the posture from whatever came previously helps to prepare people and give them a sense that something different is about to happen.

1 Put your hands in front of you, one on top of another, forming a cup (as if you were holding a butterfly inside). Think about something that is getting in the way of you worshipping. Perhaps a worry or thoughts that have been flying around your mind?

2 Hold the cup of your hands further away from your body as if you are giving that thing to God.

3 Then open your hands with the palms facing downwards and imagine that thing falling away from you to the floor.

4 Turn the palms of your hands upwards and ask the Holy Spirit to come and help you to worship.

These actions can be repeated more than once. For example the first time you might want to imagine any worries in your hands and ask the Holy Spirit to give you peace. The second time you might want to imagine distractions in your hands and ask God to

give you a sense of joy and expectation of meeting him. The third time you might want to imagine something more general (eg anything that gets in the way of worship) and then ask God to give you the freedom to express yourself in worship.

ANY NUMBER

 ## 26 Come Holy Spirit (a physical prayer)

This is another prayer that is most useful at the beginning of a worship session. It is a way of inviting the Holy Spirit to come and be with us. Again it is a prayer that can be made sitting, kneeling or standing. Sometimes you may find it helpful to play or sing a chant such as 'Veni Sancte Spiritus' while you are doing this.

This prayer utilises British Sign Language, so if you have someone in your congregation who is experienced in using this language it is a good idea to get them to lead this session.

1 *Come* – make a beckoning sign with both your hands.

3 *Spirit* – hold your right arm up and make a teardrop shape sideways across your face with the thinnest part of the teardrop at the right.

If you have someone who knows British Sign Language in your congregation you could ask them to teach you other simple repetitive prayers. Try not to make them too long or complicated though, as some people will not be able to learn the signs if the 'sentences' are too long.

2 *Holy* – hold your left palm out flat and make a fist with your right hand. Scrub the left palm with the fist of your right hand.

27 God be with me (a physical prayer)

This prayer needs a little bit more room. It is best if everyone is standing and that they have enough space to stretch their arms out. With a little practice you will find that the sections 'flow' beautifully and from that point of view it is a very good physical prayer to do. We first wrote it as an accompaniment to a song based on an old Celtic prayer:

I rest this night with God and God will rest with me.
I rest this night with Christ and Christ will rest with me.
I rest this night with the Spirit and the Spirit will rest with me.
God and Christ and the Spirit be lying down with me.

You may decide to use the Celtic version at the end of an evening service. But you can use the following variation on the prayer at any time.

God be with me – make a triangle out of both your hands and place in front of your chest. (The triangle is a symbol for the Trinity.)

Christ be with me – stretch your arms out sideways in a cross shape (the cross being a symbol for Christ).

Spirit be with me – raise both your hands. Rest them above your head and make a flame shape (like a tongue of fire, a symbol of the Holy Spirit).

Finally, bring your hands together (prayer-style) in front of your chest and begin again. Repeat as many times as you like.

The Celtic night-prayer variation

I rest this night with God and God will rest with me – make a triangle out of both your hands and place in front of your chest.

I rest this night with Christ and Christ will rest with me – stretch your arms out sideways in a cross shape.

I rest this night with the Spirit and the Spirit will rest with me – raise both your hands. Rest them above your head and make a flame shape.

God and Christ and the Spirit be lying down with me – go from 'triangle' to 'cross' to 'flame' and then finally bring your hands together prayer-style in front of your chest.

28 Patrick's breastplate (a physical prayer)

ANY NUMBER

This is a physical version of part of 'Patrick's breastplate', a very old and well-known Celtic prayer. You will need a little room for this prayer and, although it is possible to do this sitting down, it is best performed standing up.

Christ be with me – place flat hands palms together in praying position then bring arms out palms upward in a welcoming gesture.

Christ before me – praying hands then hands, palms out, in front.

Christ behind me – praying hands then hands, palms out, behind back.

Christ in me – praying hands then hands pointing inwards. Draw down body.

Christ beneath me – praying hands then, still kneeling, place palms of hands on floor.

Christ above me – praying hands, then place hands above head, palms upwards.

Christ on my right side – praying hands then right hand, palm up, moves downward.

Christ on my left side – praying hands then left hand, palm up, moves downward.

Christ in the quiet – praying hands then hands over ears.

Christ in the danger – praying hands then arms crossed outwards in a gesture of protection.

Christ in the mouth of a friend or a stranger – praying hands, then hands crossed over mouth, then hands outstretched, first narrowly then more widely.

 ANY NUMBER

29 Our Father I (a physical prayer)

This is such a well-known prayer that sometimes it goes over our heads. We say the words but we don't think about the meaning of them. The next two prayer ideas are just a couple of ways to help us notice the thoughts behind the lines of this wonderful prayer.

Resources
No special resources are needed for this, apart from the words of the prayer, perhaps on OHP.

Method
This version of the Lord's Prayer has physical actions to go with each of the lines in the prayer.

Our Father in heaven – hands open, waist height.

Hallowed be your name – raise hands in the air in a 'praising' position.

Your kingdom come – hands together in petition.

Your will be done on earth as in heaven – kneel or lie prostrate.

Give us today our daily bread – get up if lying prostrate. (Place your hands in a cup as if receiving Communion.)

Forgive us our sins – make a fist with your hand and beat breast – gently!

As we forgive those who sin against us – open fist and stretch hand outwards.

Lead us not into temptation but deliver us from evil – arms crossed over breast with hands on shoulders as if protecting chest.

For the kingdom, the power and the glory are yours – hands stretched in the air in a praising position.

30 Our Father II: super-slow style

ANY NUMBER

This is another method of helping us to reflect on the meaning of the words of the Lord's Prayer.

Resources
No special resources are needed apart from the words to the prayer.

Method
Explain that we are going to say the Lord's Prayer super-slow style and that there is going to be a pause while we let the different shades of meaning behind each line sink in. Appoint a reader to say each line of the prayer, whilst you repeat it but make sure that the reader leaves a pause of about six seconds at the end of each line of the prayer

so that the congregation has a chance to think about the meaning.

Leader: *Our Father in heaven*
Congregation: *Our Father in heaven*
(six second pause)
Leader: *Hallowed be your name*
Congregation: *Hallowed be your name*
(six second pause)
Leader: *Your kingdom come*
Congregation: *Your kingdom come*
etc.

One thing to bear in mind is to make sure that the leader has the words printed out to read. It can be difficult to say the prayer off by heart when it is being interrupted in this way.

UP TO 60/ADAPTABLE

31 Mirrors

This method of prayer can be used with a whole congregation at once, but I first experienced it as an 'installation' at a service where members of the congregation travelled between different prayer stations at their own pace. If you use it this way write the script down and place near the baptismal font. It is probably worth mentioning that if you have visually impaired people in your group this method of prayer would not be appropriate.

Resources
You will need: a selection of small, waterproof mirrors. (Mirror tiles are ideal for this. You might wish to cut them into three sections with a tile cutter to save expense.); the church font or a large bowl of water; a spotlight trained upon the font (optional).

Method
Give a mirror to everyone in the congregation who wishes to participate and then appoint a good reader to read the following script.

The mirrors script
Look into your mirror at yourself. We do this so many times in our lives. Sometimes it's for the sake of tidiness. Sometimes it's purely vanity. Sometimes it becomes our enemy as we see all the things we hate about ourselves. But now, take a long hard look in it without

vanity, without false modesty, without fear, and ask God to show you how he sees you. (Pause)

Look into your eyes. No one has had fingerprints like yours, and no one has had eyes quite like yours. The retina at the back of your eye is unique, just like a fingerprint. You are a unique human being and God loves you. (Pause)

Now look at some part of yourself you don't like in the mirror. We all have things we would like to change – things that make us feel inferior. Now ask God how he feels about this part of you. Ask to see it through his eyes. God's idea of beauty isn't the same as ours. Jesus said, 'Look how the wild flowers grow: they do not work or make clothes for themselves. But I tell you that not even King Solomon with all his wealth had clothes as beautiful as one of these flowers. It is God who clothes the wild grass – grass that is here today and gone tomorrow, burnt up in the oven. Won't he be all the more sure to clothe you?' (Matthew 6:28–30 GNB) (Pause)

Now look at some part of your body you feel you have wronged or mistreated in some way. (Pause) St Paul said: 'If one part of the body suffers, all the other parts suffer with it; if one part is praised, all the other parts share its happiness' (1 Corinthians 12:26 GNB). Apologise to God for mistreating this unique part of his creation. And if you can, make a resolution to be kinder to yourself in future. (Pause)

St Paul said we all entered the same body – Christ's body – when we were baptised. And we were given the same drink, the Holy Spirit. We're all part of a larger body, and everything we do affects it too. Look at yourself in the mirror once more, imagining that you are not alone. You are part of a bigger body, a larger, smiling face, an open, loving hand. And if you feel you can, then take your mirror and drop it in the font as a sign that you are washing away all your fears, pride, hang-ups and prejudices about your body, and joining a large, loving body that will never grow old or fade away.

32 Salt

We did this meditation as part of a series of services based on the Sermon on the Mount.

Resources
You will need: a bowl of salt (dishwasher salt works best because of its large grains, but don't eat it!); an atlas open at the 'world' page (or a large poster of the same thing laid on the floor).

Method
Pour some of the salt into a bowl and pass the bowl around the congregation. Invite them to take some salt out of the bowl and keep it in their hands. Appoint a reader to read the following short script.

The salt script
Jesus said, 'You are the salt for all mankind. But if salt loses its saltiness there is no way to make it salty again. It has become worthless, so it is thrown out and people trample on it.' (Matthew 5:13 GNB)

Let's now have a short time when we think about what it means to be the salt of the earth – the salt that spices up all humanity. (Short pause) Who might God want us to spice? (Pause) Where should we be spreading our salt? (Pause) Have we lost our edge? (Pause) Or are we spreading salt where there is plenty already, leaving one dish over-spiced and another empty? (Longer pause)

After the script you may want to give the congregation the opportunity to say the following prayer (which could be photocopied or put on slide or OHP).

Lord we resolve to be salt to a bland world
To spice up lives that are lonely or bland
To heal the wounded and oppose those who
    wound
To flavour humanity with love and good news
To cover dark ugliness with white shining
    beauty.

After this invite the congregation to come up and place their grains of salt over the map of the world as part of their resolution to be salt in a saltless world.

33 A prayer labyrinth

UP TO 60

This is a method of prayer and listening to God that we have found most helpful. We now use it regularly, once a month. The reason we have found it so good is that many of us have busy, stressful lives, and performing a simple action, like walking a pathway to help prepare ourselves to pray and listen to God, can be a good way of getting rid of all the shopping lists, family arguments and worries about money that buzz around our heads and distract us when we are trying to pray.

Labyrinths were a feature of many medieval cathedrals, most famously in Chartres cathedral in France, although people have been making them since long before Christ was born. They were probably adopted by the church due to their cross-like symmetry which reminded people of the journey Christ made to be crucified.

A labyrinth of this sort has no walls. It is marked on the floor and, unlike a maze, has only one path. There are no tricks so you can't get lost. Not all labyrinths have cross-shaped symmetry but the Christian versions are generally based on this cross shape. The idea was that a person would walk the labyrinth on the eve of their baptism, confirmation, or before Easter as an aid to contemplative prayer and reflection.

As you wind your way round, approaching the centre, you gradually offload the pressures of the day. You can also view it as an allegory of your life, sometimes appearing to

be close to God, only to be thrown out to the edge suddenly, or perhaps to find yourself walking in sympathy with others, and at other times far distant from them.

At the centre you can sit and rest in God's presence for as long as you like. Then you walk the labyrinth outwards, carrying the light of Christ with you out into the world.

We like to ensure that the atmosphere of the space surrounding the labyrinth is conducive to contemplation – we are lucky enough to have a medieval building to lay ours in. We play plainchant over a small sound system to cover up the noise of the traffic outside, and we have candles and Bibles around. It is a quiet, sacred space, devoted to prayer and to listening to God.

Resources

You will need: a labyrinth of some sort. (These can be made in a number of different ways – see the 'how to make a labyrinth' section below); plenty of candles (stood in seed trays full of wet sand to make the building seem more welcoming); a small stereo playing gentle plainchant music can be helpful; plenty of Bibles. (They can be available around the building and in the centre of the labyrinth for people to read if they wish.)

During the Easter season (perhaps on Good Friday) you may also wish to have 'props' from the Easter story situated around the labyrinth for people to pass, eg a crown of thorns, a purple robe, dice, a whip, red flower petals (to symbolise blood), nails, an INRI sign, a sponge, a spear. We recommend dimming the lights and using a spotlight on the labyrinth if you have one.

How to make a labyrinth

The resources you will need depend on what materials you wish to make a labyrinth out of. You can make a transitory one using almost any material such as ribbon, toilet tissue or stones. However making these involves a lot of hard work so we recommend the following methods.

1 Paint on the floor (get advice from a DIY shop as to what paint is the best for your surface). This is best in buildings where the floor isn't particularly old or beautiful, such as a church hall. If you use this method you will have to think carefully about the other uses this building is put to and whether the labyrinth might interfere with them.

2 White tape such as 'gaffer' or insulating tape on a mat, some linoleum or a large piece of material, perhaps canvas. This method is my favourite and has the advantage that you may take your labyrinth anywhere, and roll it up when it isn't needed.

3 If you are lucky enough to have a large garden you may decide to make a labyrinth outside. The path could be marked using large white stones, flowerbeds, or gravel.

Pattern 1 – The Chartres Labyrinth

Pattern 2 – An alternative for a smaller room.

Now you can start the drawing. First you decide where you want the entrance to be and mark a large cross shape, the same diameter as the labyrinth on the floor in pencil. (If you're doing this on cloth just fold the cloth in quarters and iron creases into it.)

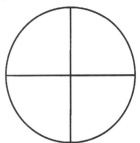

The lines will intersect where you want the middle of the labyrinth to be. The 'bottom' of the cross will be where the entrance will be. Make sure you don't do this in paint as it is only your 'working out' and you're going to rub bits of it out later. Beside the bottom of the cross, do two lines the width of your path (eg 1 foot wide for our 28 ft example) going to the centre of the cross (see diagram below).

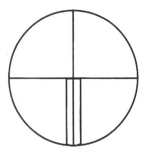

Then you have to draw the circles. The best way to do these is to get a big tin or coffee jar, a huge circle of string and a pencil (to use as a giant pair of compasses). You will draw 12 circles in all. So, to use our 28 ft example, the first thing you would do is set the string to 3 ft long and draw the middle circle. Then set the string to 4 ft long to do the second circle. Carry on until the last circle when the string is set to 14 ft.

(Don't draw the circle across the two paths by the entrance if you can help it. If you accidentally do this, make sure it is in pencil so you can rub it out later.)

Nearly there now! Look at pattern 1 carefully. Some of the paths do u-turns on themselves. At these points rub out little bits of the circle to allow the path to curve round on itself. At other points rub out the cross so that the path can just go around the circle uninterrupted. Walk round it to check that you've rubbed out the right bits and that you can get to the centre without hitting a dead end. Then just go over the labyrinth with paint or tape, or whatever you want to make the marks permanent, and you're finished.

If you haven't got enough space to make a Chartres Labyrinth you may decide to use pattern 2 instead. You will have to modify any notes you give out at the entrance to the labyrinth accordingly, but you will have more room for walkers to pass one another, or spend time in the middle of the labyrinth if they wish, without being disturbed.

Opening your labyrinth for prayer

When you first have your labyrinth open, it is a good idea to copy the handout on the following page (or something similar to this) and place it on a sheet near the entrance to the labyrinth. This saves you having to explain what is happening in words and disturbing others' prayer in the process. As you can see from these instructions, we usually ask people to remove their shoes before walking. This actually serves a practical purpose. As well as being a spiritual preparation exercise it also helps to keep the mat clean. Also, we usually have a clipboard available at the entrance to the labyrinth if people wish to share any thoughts with others. It is also a good idea to place 'silence' notices at the front of the church to prevent distractions. The labyrinth actually works best when it isn't too crowded with people so you might want to consider a way of encouraging people to stagger their entrances.

You may also wish to have some people on hand to pray or talk with people if they need to weigh up something they think God has said to them. This is best done a short distance away where the sound will not disturb those praying.

Other variations:
I – Singing a labyrinth

You might like to try singing a labyrinth sometime. To do this you will need everyone to arrive at the same time, unlike normally, when staggered entrances work better. Choose a simple song, one you all know well and don't need the words for. 'Rounds' work very well for this: 'Jubilate Deo' by Taizé is a good example if you know it.

If you are singing a 'round' arrange beforehand which people are going to sing which parts and then enter the labyrinth. As you enter, begin singing your song. The beautiful thing about this is that the sound moves as the people move and you hear different voices as you draw near to different people in the group.

II – Dancing a labyrinth

In the Middle Ages people sometimes danced around labyrinths on church feast days. This was usually on labyrinths that were situated outdoors. The dancers held hands until they were in a long line, and then the whole line entered the labyrinth, skipping in time to some dance music that was being played by musicians outside. You might like to try this yourself – you could even combine it with the singing idea above.

UNDER 20

34 Circles

This is a way of praying for each other. It works best when the group isn't too large and has enough space to form a circle without feeling squashed. Sometimes we use this method of prayer before the congregation has arrived for a service, as a sort of preparation for ourselves.

Resources

No special resources are needed.

Method

Ask everyone who wishes to participate to form a circle, holding hands. While you are still holding hands, ask the Holy Spirit to come and be with you. Then ask everyone to turn to pray for the person on their left. You can do this by remaining holding hands if you wish, or you may like to invite everyone to turn to their left and place their hands on the shoulders, head or back of the person to their left while they are doing this. Then, after a little while, ask everyone to turn and pray for the person on their right. Finally, ask everyone in the circle to turn completely, until they are facing outwards and hold hands in a ring once more. Then pray for the city, or perhaps pray for those people thinking of coming to the service, or even pray for world situations. You may wish to finish with 'The Grace'.

The history of Chartres Labyrinth

This labyrinth is a smaller copy of a labyrinth laid on the floor of Chartres Cathedral in France in about the year 1220. The difference between a maze and a labyrinth is that a labyrinth has only one pathway. It has no dead ends, so it is impossible to get lost.

Medieval Christian labyrinth designs usually had two main characteristics. They were based on an equal-armed cross shape and usually had some rotational symmetry. In medieval times the labyrinth, with its twisting and tortuous path, was used to symbolise the journey to the Holy Land, or the journey Christ took to the cross. In Chartres Cathedral, pilgrims who were going to be baptised or confirmed the next day walked the labyrinth on their knees (which as the original was made of stone must have been quite painful).

What is it for and why do it?
The labyrinth is just a prayer and meditation aid. They have been used for thousands of years in different places to help people to forget the hassles of their everyday lives and draw close to God. Sometimes it's hard just to 'Be still and know that I am God.' (Psalm 46:10) Sitting still and listening can often lead you to fall asleep! Walking slowly around something like this can help because your feet are occupied with a gentle repetitive task giving the rest of you time and space to pray. The labyrinth also symbolises our journey to heaven. You will notice that there are times on the journey when you feel very near to the centre, and times when you think you will never get there or that you must have gone the wrong way. But as long as you stay on the path you will not go wrong.

'Show me your ways, O Lord,
teach me your paths; guide me in your truth and teach me,
for you are God my Saviour' (Psalm 25:4,5).

Before entering the labyrinth you may find it might help just to sit and be still for a little while. Please take off your shoes (you can leave your socks on) as Moses did when he listened to the voice of God in the burning bush: 'Take off your sandals for the place where you are standing is holy ground.' (Exodus 3:5)

The first stage of the journey is letting go – giving all the details of your life to God: 'Cast all your anxiety on him because he cares for you.' (1 Peter 5:7)

The second stage of the journey is receiving whatever God wishes to give to you in the centre of the labyrinth. Spend as long as you like there, as Mary did when she sat at Jesus' feet listening to him (Luke 10:38–42). The centre of this labyrinth seats two people.

The third stage of the journey is going back into the world, bringing the Light of Christ with you.

Some purely practical points
Feel free to walk at your own pace as slowly or as fast as you like. If someone wishes to pass you in the other direction, just step to one side (keeping your place on the right track with a toe or two). If you have received any prophecies, Bible verses, pictures from God, etc that you would like to share with others then there will be a clipboard and pencil near the entrance.

35 Reviewing the day

This prayer technique was started by St Ignatius of Loyola, but since then many different people have written variations upon this. Here are just a few of them.

Resources
None are really needed but you may find a pen and a blank diary or notebook to be helpful. If you are doing this with children you may wish to use a drawing book and crayons.

Method
This is a prayer method that is at its most effective when used daily. We have done variations upon this a few times as part of an evening service, but this present version is my favourite at the moment.

First find a position that you feel comfortable with and ask God's Holy Spirit to come and be with you. You might decide to do a breathing prayer to help you with this. Ask God to prompt your thoughts as you do the next two parts.

Sit and think of five things you want to thank God for, that have happened that day. You may wish to write these down or draw them with the crayons. Spend some time just being thankful for these things, then move onto the next section.

Ask the Holy Spirit to bring one event of the day to mind. Something that if you could change the way you dealt with it, you would. You probably won't want to write this bit in your diary as it might dredge up unhelpful guilty feelings later. Talk to God about that event. If you feel you should apologise to God about it then do so, but do not go on a big 'guilt trip' about it. Talk to God about other ways you could have dealt with the event and resolve next time to deal with it in the 'new ways' you have just thought about.

You may then wish to put the resolution in your diary, or not, depending on what the resolution was.

If you do this as a diary, every so often you may want to look back and thank God for the last month or two.

There are many different approaches to this way of prayer. You may decide to just concentrate on one thing to be thankful for each day. Or you may decide to connect it more to the way you behaved that day, and think of your most Christlike and least Christlike or loving actions that day. Whatever way you decide to do this, however, make it a positive event, not a 'guilt trip'.

36 Consequences

This first version of this prayer is best done in a group where you know each other fairly well. A small-group situation would be best. It probably will not work if there is someone you don't know at all in the group, as they will feel left out.

The second variation can be used with any group of people (although with large numbers you are best limiting the number of paper folds to around five).

Resources
Some long pieces of paper (A4 would be fine); pens. If you want to save money you may cut each sheet of paper into 3 strips lengthways.

Method
Give a piece of paper to each person and ask them to fold the paper as many times as there are people present in the group, starting at the bottom of the sheet. Then ask them to put their name at the top of the sheet. Unfold the pieces again and pass the pieces of paper around the group, asking each member to write a down a talent or gift of the person named at the top of the paper. It can be a practical talent, or a more spiritual talent. Emphasise that the things written should all be very positive things that will encourage the named person and the whole group.

As in the game 'Consequences', fold down your piece of paper when you have written something, and pass it on. Try not to be too obvious all the time. For example, the church organist might be a little bored receiving a piece of paper saying 'musical' ten times.

You may decide to do this section of the prayer in silence so that people can quietly ask God to prompt them to put the right thing for each person.

When all the pieces of paper have been written, give them to the named people and let them read what people have put. When all the pieces of paper have been read, place them in the middle of the group and have a time of thanking God for all our gifts and talents and asking him to help us to develop our talents and use them well.

When you have finished praying, allow everyone to take their piece of paper home with them.

Variation: Blessing consequences
A variation on this method that will work with any group, is to write blessings upon the pieces of paper. You could use Bible verses for these blessings, or perhaps use Celtic blessings or blessings in your own words. (You may wish to have Bibles and a concordance available for people to look up anything they can't quite remember.)

37 Patchwork

UP TO 60

This is a method of prayer we used at our Easter Communion service. We used it to make a patchwork altar cloth. You may decide to use it to make another item. In a Morning Prayer or Family Service you may want to make a large patchwork cross. An alternative would be to make a human figure out of your patchwork as a symbol that, together, we all make up the body of Christ.

Resources
You will need: a collection of many different pieces of material, large or small, with many different types of pattern upon them; several pairs of scissors (as you may be worried about frayed edges, pinking shears would be best for this or if you pre-cut the squares you could iron the edges down so that when they are stuck no frayed edges are seen); PVA glue or perhaps needles and shiny gold thread if you wish to tack the pieces to the backing instead of gluing them, or you could use pins if you wished; a backing piece of material cut to the shape of the finished piece.

Method
This method of prayer is best worked alongside something else going on in the same building at the same time, for example, during a period of sung worship. Otherwise it can be difficult to get everyone around the cloth at once. Ask each person to come up to the front of the church, in their own time, and choose a piece of material that they feel suits their personality, or how they are feeling at the moment. (You can make this ritual still more complex by having fabric pens available too.) You may want to pre-cut the fabric squares if you want to get them even, or you may ask people to cut the squares themselves, in any shape they wish, also to describe themselves and how they are feeling.

When they come to tack or stick the squares on the cloth, encourage people to use this as a prayer, offering themselves and their feelings to God. When the cloth is finished, you might want to display it in some way. If you are making an altar cloth you could process it up the church to place on the Communion table. If you have made some other figure you may wish to hang it from a banner pole or attach it to some sort of stand for all to see. You could have some gesture of acknowledgement, perhaps by praying a finishing prayer, by gently sprinkling holy water on the patchwork, or by (carefully!) incensing it using a thurible.

Variation – The weaving prayer

Resources
You will need: a large piece of coloured paper; long strips of different coloured papers (preferably colours that blend with the first colour); a knife; a ruler; pencils or pens.

This variation uses paper instead of cloth. Cut your initial altar cloth or symbol out of coloured paper. Then with a craft or Stanley knife carefully cut parallel slits in the paper. Cut other long strips of different coloured papers for people to choose (many unusual and beautiful colours are available these days from art shops or good stationers). Allow people, not only to choose a piece of coloured paper to weave, but also to write anything they wish on the back of their piece of paper. Have pencils or pens available.

 38 Photographs

UNDER 20

This is a method of intercession for members of the group that are not present for some reason. Perhaps they are working abroad on a missionary or aid project and you want to show your support, or maybe they are ill. We are all different and some people might not appreciate being prayed for in this way, so check it out with them or with someone who knows them well first.

Resources
You will need: a good quality photograph; a piece of stiff, good quality card, larger than the photograph; PVA glue; a pen (a black ink-based pen would work best); a clipboard would also come in useful.

Method
Choose a really nice photo of the person or people to be prayed for. Perhaps get a person in the church who is talented at producing a good photo to take one. Using the glue, mount the photograph on the card so that it forms a frame with a nice thick border around the photo. Then, during a time of silent prayer, pass the photo and the pen around the church. It is a good idea to pass around some information about the person as well, for

example a prayer letter. Ask people to pray for the person (or people) and when they have been prayed for, ask people to sign the photo frame. When everyone has finished, you could perhaps send this photo to the person as a gift, to show you have been thinking of them.

Variations
More than one of these photos can be passed around during a silent prayer session. You could also pray for items in the news by mounting newspaper articles or photos on card and sending them around the church. (Of course, you probably wouldn't want to send these anywhere, but you could display them somewhere afterwards.)

Another variation on this is to have individual photos of everyone in the group (perhaps ask each person to bring one for the following week). Then pass all these photos around at once. As you receive someone's photo, silently pray for that person, until everyone has been prayed for.

 39 Props

UNDER 20

This method of prayer is more suitable with a smaller size of group – either a prayer group or a small congregation of probably no more than about fifteen to twenty people. It is good for groups of people who don't really like praying out loud. They can pray silently but we all still know who they are praying for.

Resources
You will need: a selection of 'props' brought by individual members of the congregation. (You will need to remind everyone to bring something with them the week before.) A small coffee table might be useful to place the props on.

Method
The week before the prayer session, ask each person to bring something with them the next week that represents something they are worried about and would like prayer for. For example, if someone was worried about their child they might bring one of his toys with

them. If they are having problems at work, they might bring a sheet of office notepaper with them. If a friend is ill, a thermometer might be brought. If guidance is needed about an issue, they might bring a map with them. The item can be anything they wish to bring. It might be obvious or more obscure.

At the meeting the following week, seat everyone in a loose circle around the coffee table. (Create a space on the carpet if you have no table.) Allow each person in turn to say what they want to about their item. It might be a long explanation or it might be quite short: 'My auntie is very ill'. After each explanation ask the person to place their item on the table in the middle of the room.

When everyone has explained their items, have a time of silent prayer. Encourage each person, as they are praying for an issue, to pick up the item connected to that issue. Everyone in the group then knows who is being prayed for even though the person may be praying silently. Finish the prayer time when everyone has finished picking up the items.

 ### 40 Sand

UNDER 20

This prayer ritual is best used as an installation while other things are going on, perhaps at an Easter or Lent service. But place the installation in a quiet place so people have the time and the space to think. Of course if you are lucky enough to live by a beach you might decide to try it, or some variation on it, there instead.

Resources

You will need: a sand pit (cheap plastic ones can be bought at any good toyshop, or you could make one. Watch out for splinters though!); sand (play sand can be bought from toy shops or garden centres); a piece of hardboard to smooth the sand afterwards; a washing up bowl of water and a towel nearby. You may wish to protect your floor with plastic or newspapers too.

Method

Fill the sandpit with sand, and wet the sand with a little warm water so it's gently damp. Then copy the following text and place nearby (one copy for each person participating). You could even make a tape of the text if you wished and give people the opportunity to play it on a tape recorder with headphones.

The sand text

Take your shoes and socks off and step onto the sand. Dig your toes into it till your feet sink deeply in, making a print. Take your feet off the place where they have been standing and look down at the footprints. What do they remind you of? Perhaps you might like to kneel down and examine them closely, perhaps touching them gently, following the curves, the shape of the toes, the hollows and lines that are as individual as a fingerprint. Perhaps they remind you of the poem about footprints in the sand.

Maybe they remind you of the prints of hands and feet in the concrete pavement in Hollywood. The prints of rich and famous people.

Perhaps they remind you of tracks in the snow. Have you ever followed anyone else's tracks in the snow or their footprints on a sandy beach?

Are there human beings whose tracks you follow metaphorically? People you admire? People you want to be like – your heroes? Think about these people for a few minutes.

Imagine yourself following them in the desert now. Where are they leading you? To a good place or a bad one? An oasis or a valley of bones? Do they make you a better human being or a worse one?

Now imagine you are on a sandy beach by a lake. A figure is standing there. You hear him call to you, 'Come follow me and I will teach you to fish for people.' What do you say to the figure? Are you ready to follow him? Tell him what you feel about his question.

Now, if you feel it is appropriate, kneel looking at the sand and imagine you are kneeling at Jesus' feet on that beach. Tell him what you have discovered through this journey. Tell him your fears, your hopes, your discoveries about your heroes and where you think they might lead you.

When you have finished praying about this, take a piece of board and wipe away your footprint till the sand is smooth once more. Then wash your feet.

41 Absolution

ANY NUMBER

This is our variation on Asperges (an ancient ritual of blessing and forgiveness). It works particularly well after a confession time, especially one that has been quite detailed, unusual or powerful in some way. Sometimes a very powerful confession time can somehow leave some people still feeling guilty. This is a good way of reassuring them that God has forgiven them and making them feel more positive.

Resources
You will need: some small finger bowls full of water, and some volunteers.

Method
Traditionally, holy water is used and the priest 'sprinkles' the congregation. We like to be more informal than this. We still have the priest pronouncing an absolution from the front of the church, but the volunteers are just ordinary members of the congregation. We like to have enough volunteers to make sure that no one in the church is missed out.

When the absolution is said, the volunteers go around the congregation, gently and lightly sprinkling them on the head with water from their fingertips. Try and cover everyone in the building so that everyone has the chance to feel special and forgiven. Also, be very careful to only use a very tiny amount of water. Some people might be a little upset at having their hair soaked. You might decide to say some special words of some sort as you sprinkle people's heads or you might decide to sing a song about forgiveness as this ritual is performed.

42 An Easter offering

ANY NUMBER

This is designed as an offertory ritual and prayer for an Easter Communion service, to remind us of details of the crucifixion story and how much Christ loves us.

Resources
You will need: a crown of thorns; some dice and a vest; a sponge full of vinegar; a whip; some nails; some pieces of silver (this may be the collection plate); bread and wine.

Method
When the service is being planned, ask for some volunteers to take these items in procession to the altar or Communion table, one at a time, and to pray the following prayers (or something similar) as they do so. As a purely practical point, in a large building make sure that a microphone is placed nearby so that everyone can hear the prayers as the people bring the items to the table.

1st person (a crown of thorns)
I bring a crown of thorns to the table to remind us of the King who ruled from a cross. May we always follow his example and lead by serving one another in love.

2nd person (a whip)
I bring a whip to the table to remind us of the Sacrifice who let his back be striped with blood so that we could be healed. May we always look for your healing and spread it to comfort a suffering world.

3rd person (dice and a vest)
I bring dice to the table to remind us of the Generous One who was stripped naked in love. He gave everything he had for us. Help us to be generous to him, and to each other.

4th person (a sponge full of vinegar)
I bring a sponge to the table to remind us of a thirsty man. May we always be thirsty for justice and the kingdom of heaven.

5th person (some nails)
I bring nails to the table to remind us of a loving

heart, full of forgiveness, who, as the nails were hammered into him prayed for his torturers. Give us the power to forgive as he did.

6th person (pieces of silver)
I bring silver to the table to remind us of God sold for the price of a slave. May we always use our money wisely and never hurt another human being with it.

7th person (bread)
I bring bread to the table to remind us of the strong body of the Messiah, weakening and dying on the cross. Help us use whatever strength we have to serve him.

8th person (wine)
I bring wine to the table to remind us of the blood of Christ flowing from an unselfish heart. May our selfishness die, and be replaced with everlasting love.

ANY NUMBER

43 Remembrance

This ritual is designed for Remembrance Sunday. We were trying to find a way of making this day more personal and meaningful to those people who don't remember the two World Wars.

Resources
You will need: barbed wire; pictures from newspapers or magazines; poppies; photographs of some local people or soldiers who were killed in one of the wars (you should be able to obtain information from your local library or members of your own congregation); candles; a piece of poetry or extract from a book describing what it was like to live in wartime.

Method
You may find that this remembrance ritual gets quite emotional, as it has the effect of making these tragedies more real and less like statistics. Be aware of this, and structure the way this is presented to allow people to show any grief they are feeling without embarrassment, for example, by having the lighting fairly low, or by having everyone facing the front rather than in a circle.

Create a large ring of barbed wire, reminiscent of a crown of thorns, at the front of the church. Place poppies at regular intervals in the wire. What follows next depends on the information that you have found. Try and balance events from the world wars with more recent events in the news. Also include events involving civilians or children. Ask different people to come up to the circle of barbed wire, carrying a picture or a news article. You may wish to put these in a stand-up frame so they can be more easily seen. Write a short script for each person to say, and after each person has come up have a little pause for prayer. (I've made up these scripts with mostly fictional information to give you an idea of the sort of thing you can do.)

1st person (First World War)
Here is a picture of Stephen Smith, killed in the First World War, at the battle of the Somme. He lived near here in Haxby and was only 19 when he died. We remember him, and everyone like him who suffered.

2nd person (Second World War)
Here is a picture of Alan Jones, killed in the Second World War, in Italy. Before the war he worked in a chocolate factory near here, and when he died he left a wife and three children. We remember him, and everyone like him who suffered.

3rd person (civilian victims of the wars)
Here is a picture of a local convent during the war. When it was bombed, five nuns died. We remember them and all civilian victims of war.

4th person (landmines)
Here is a picture of Bosnian children, maimed by landmines. We pray for them and we remember everyone who has been injured or killed by these terrible weapons.

5th person (Northern Ireland)
Here is a picture of a bombed pub in Belfast. We remember everyone who died there so suddenly, and all the casualties of terrorism. We pray now for their families.

6th person (a red rose)
Here is a red rose, symbol of love. We

remember everyone who has lost someone they loved through war. We pray for healing from the pain, and for new purpose and happiness to come into their lives sometime soon.

7th person (recent news article)
Here is a picture from … where they are fighting right now. We pray that this war would soon stop and peace would come to this country. We pray for the casualties and those who are suffering so much through this.

When you have finished these prayers read the extract from the book or poem about war. Then, finally, give people a chance to place more poppies and candles around the barbed wire circle.

44 Short prayers

Prayers like these are better known in the Orthodox or Catholic traditions. Short repeated prayers can be very helpful, in helping to focus ourselves on prayer, or in everyday situations when we are nervous and just wish to ask God to be with us. They are sometimes called mantras. Sadly, this name generates mistrust in certain Christian circles, due to its association with Buddhism, yet, unlike a Buddhist mantra which is about emptying your brain, these short, simple prayers are about asking God to fill us, be with us, or teach us something new from Scripture.

Resources
No special resources are needed so you can try these prayers anywhere.

Method
When using any of these prayers in public worship, explain a little about the prayer and where it comes from (eg from Scripture, or the Orthodox tradition). We have found that when we have used these prayers in public worship we have found it helpful to play some gentle but rhythmic music behind them, so that people can 'pace' the prayer. The end of the piece of music also gives a good end point for the prayer so the congregation knows when to stop.

The Jesus prayer
This prayer is widely used in the Orthodox tradition. I have encountered a few different versions of it, but the basic gist is the same in each.

Lord Jesus Christ, Son of the Living God, have mercy on me, a sinner.

A shorter version that I like to use, due to its brevity and rhythmic lilt, is:

Jesus Christ, Son of God, have mercy on me.

The idea is to repeat the prayer often, until its meaning sinks into you. I find this prayer to be particularly helpful in everyday life when encountering a difficult situation.

Other short prayers

Abba Father

Jesus used the word 'Abba' to address God. It means 'Father' in Aramaic (see Mark 14:36).

You might find this prayer helpful before beginning a time of intercession.

You can also sometimes take prayers from the Bible reading for that Sunday and turn them into short repeated prayers, eg.

Rabboni (John 20:16)

My Lord and my God (John 20:28).

Increase our faith (Luke 17:5).

My soul thirsts for you (Psalm 63:1).

Trust in the Lord and do good (Psalm 37:3).

Sometimes simple question and answer prayers can be repeated too. Below is a prayer we used in a service which was loosely based on the reading from John when Jesus reinstates Peter (John 21:15–18).

Voice 1: *Do you love me?*
Voice 2: *I love you.*
Voice 1: *Do you trust me?*
Voice 2: *I trust you.*

Sometimes it can be very powerful to take a simple phrase from a Bible reading and repeat it, thoughtfully, until its meaning sinks in:

I am the bread of life (John 6:48).

Be still, and know that I am God (Psalm 46:10).

Come, follow me (Matthew 4:19).

I am the way and the truth and the life (John 14:6).

`UP TO 60/ADAPTABLE`

45 Fruit

We first did a fruit meditation as part of a service on the Holy Spirit at Pentecost. Our congregation really seemed to appreciate being able to choose different fruits and to be able to eat them at the end of the meditation.

Resources
You will need: a bowl of different kinds of fruit; some little side plates and knives (they might come in handy).

Method
Pass the fruitbowl (or fruitbowls if you have a large congregation) around the church and let people choose a fruit for themselves. Have a good selection of many different types, ranging from the large to the very small (such as grapes) and from the mundane to the exotic. Then appoint a good reader to read the following script.

The fruit script
Take your fruit and look at it carefully. Look at the colours within the fruit and notice how they vary according to the light and shadows. Touch it and feel its skin. Is it smooth or bumpy? Look around at the other fruits you can see. So many different types. So many colours and textures. Yet they are all still fruit. Jesus said, 'I am the vine; you are the branches. If a person remains in me and I in them, they will bear much fruit; apart from me you can do nothing.'

Think now for a minute about the sorts of fruit you might bear.

Love? (Pause) *Joy?* (Pause) *Patience?* (Pause) *Kindness?* (Pause)

Perhaps your fruit might not be the sort of thing you would think of straightaway as being fruit. It might be exotic. It might be mundane. Maybe it's making tasty meals for others, providing a listening ear or sharing a computer program that helps other people do their accounts. Cut into your fruit now, and taste a little. Notice its sweetness.

What do you do that makes life a little sweeter for others? Maybe that's your fruit. (Long pause)

You might be feeling a little fruitless at the moment. Or like you used to bear fruit in the past, yet somehow you're feeling a bit dry and uninspired. Or maybe you want to grow some new fruits.

Jesus compared God to the gardener who prunes the fruit tree to bear more fruit. Are there any branches of your life that seem to be going nowhere, projects you should be cutting back on? These might just need to grow a little more, or need a little more patience and love. Or maybe it's time for something new. Ask God to prompt you now, to show you the difference. Where should you be shedding old branches, old projects, and beginning new ones? (Pause)

Where should you just be asking him for more help to grow, and patience to wait for the growth to happen? Ask God to send the Holy Spirit to inspire you and bring new fruit to your life now. (Long pause)

Finish by spending some time eating your fruit. Perhaps you'd like to pass your fruit around and taste someone else's fruit too.

`ANY NUMBER`

46 Destruction

We first performed this ritual when we heard of a church that had been destroyed and the missionaries there had asked us to pray for them. We were surprised when we prayed this way just how moving it was. Suddenly it

transported the story of destruction from our heads right into our emotions.

Resources

You will need: building materials to form a simple sculpture, perhaps of a cross or an altar (we used the bricks and perspex that we sometimes use for a Communion table – see **Advent** on p18)

Method

Build your sculpture before the start of the service. It might help if it is already familiar to the congregation (perhaps used on a previous occasion). At the point where you wish to begin the prayer, read a story or some news of a church that is being persecuted, destroyed or is suffering, somewhere in the world. Then ask people to pray for that situation quietly, and as they do, send one or two people out to knock down, kick down, or destroy what you have made, as callously and irreverently as possible. (It really is emotionally shocking to be confronted with such violence in a church situation and certainly helps us understand better the sufferings of the persecuted church).

At the end of this session you may wish to have some aspect of rebuilding, either by inviting the congregation to help recreate the former sculpture, or by lighting candles around the ruins.

UP TO 60/ADAPTABLE

47 A letter to God

This method of prayer works best when plenty of time is given for the congregation to write whatever they wish in their letters. Unlike **Incense I** it is more of an expression of ourselves, our lives and how we are honestly feeling than an intercession, although the letters can eventually be dealt with by burning if that is what you wish. The most important thing about this ritual, however, is that the letters remain private and that the congregation knows this.

You will find that some people express themselves better on paper than others. When we did this ritual for the first time one person

commented that they had always found prayer difficult, until they tried this method, which was immensely helpful for them. Something to bear in mind is that this method of prayer can unlock feelings that people have been suppressing, so you might wish to have people around to pray for, or listen to, anyone who feels like this.

Resources

You will need: pens and paper (unless you are burning the pieces of paper you might like to use nice letter paper for this); sealing wax; a candle; a seal or stamp of some sort.

Method

You might like to read a passage from a book or story where someone describes how they are feeling, or a letter to God you have written yourself, as an example to inspire people. You can miss this out though, just as long as people know that they can and should be totally honest about their anger, fears, doubts etc.

Then give out the paper and the pens, and allow time for people to write their letters. You may wish to play some music or have another ritual going on at the same time, so that if some people finish earlier than others they don't get too bored. Then, when each person has finished their letter, encourage them to seal the letter with some sealing wax so it remains private and place it in a basket or box at the front of the church, perhaps in front of a cross. (If it is a Communion service you may wish to place the letters on the Communion table during the liturgy.)

What happens next depends on the resources available to you and how you wish to deal with the letters. My personal preference is to get a cardboard box or pot, and ceremonially bury them in the church garden at the end of the service. Then people will know where the letters are and that they will remain private, yet undestroyed. Other options might be burning them with incense or having them concreted or plastered into any building work that is going on in the church (although this may be less private as they might be uncovered at a later date). You may also find that some people have 'unfinished business'

and wish to take their letter home with them to pray about. That is fine and you may decide to do this with everyone, getting them to place their names on the outside of the sealed letter so that they can retrieve it again at the end of the service.

UP TO 60

48 Thanksgiving

This method is slightly more technological than some, but it is not difficult, and gives everyone who wishes to, a chance to participate in forming a corporate prayer without the embarrassment of standing at the front of the church and speaking in public.

Resources
You will need: a tape recorder, microphone and some sort of amplifier and speakers to play the finished tape during the service; a clipboard and pencil (optional). A camcorder could be used instead of a tape recorder, in which case TVs or a video projector will be needed to play the finished tape.

Method
You have to do a little forward planning for this method of prayer. You can either do it at the end of the service the week before, as people are going out, or some hours before the start of the service on the day. Remember you may need extra time to redo the tape just in case it goes wrong for any reason.

Start recording the tape by having someone say the following words, or something similar.

'Lord, today we especially want to thank you for...'

Then press 'pause' on the tape recorder while keeping it on record.

Go around the church and ask different people what they would like to put on the tape. Getting lots of different people to say just one thing can be quite effective. A clipboard and pencil will probably be handy because people may want to know what people before them have said so that they can

add new things rather than repeat old things. If you press 'pause' rather than 'stop' while recording each person you will, hopefully, not get too many annoying clicks between the different voices. Remember to record the tape somewhere without too much background noise. When you have finished the tape you can play it during a service, perhaps at the end of the intercessions.

Your resulting tape might sound something a bit like this:

Lord, today we especially want to thank you for... sunshine, the World Cup, your healing touch, salvation, hope when I'm feeling down, chocolate, you just being there, heaven, music, dancing, the television, doctors, computers, best friends, the Bible, flowers, holidays, forgiveness, church, food and clothes, a new job... etc.

The subjects on the tape may range from the deeply serious to just little things like one of the children's favourite TV programmes, but that's part of the beauty of this method of prayer – that hopefully it encompasses all the little details of our lives together.

After you have played the tape you might like everyone to say 'Amen' at the end.

Variations
This method of prayer can be used for all sorts of different subjects. You could use it for a time of intercession rather than thanksgiving. You can also 'interview' people by asking them different things. This can be handy for the teaching slot as well as the prayers. For example we once interviewed people by asking them: 'Tell us about a time when God spoke to you in some way, changing your plans.' This was very interesting because people told us of lots of different ways God had spoken to them, ranging from the very subtle to the miraculous, and in this way we learnt a lot about the other side of prayer – God communicating with us.

49 Wood

UP TO 60/ADAPTABLE

This meditation is most effective during the build-up to Easter. Some people have found it to be very moving. Others have found the hammering action to be a little disconcerting. For this reason we used it as an option during a set of 'installations' or different prayer rituals.

Resources
You will need: small pieces of wood (any sort will do really: firewood, reclaimed timber or plywood); nails; some hammers.

Method
Give out the pieces of wood, (two for each person) and the nails (one per person is probably enough). Then appoint a good reader to read the following script (or, if you are doing it as an installation, print out the script and place near to the wood and hammers).

The wood script
Pick up your piece of wood and look at it closely. Examine its grain, its colour. Being careful of splinters, gently run your fingers down its grain and feel its rough texture. Now, in your mind's eye, imagine this piece of wood sitting in a workshop in Nazareth, having just been cut off a larger block. It's waiting to be made into a new piece of furniture: a table, a chair or a smaller more delicate item. Imagine Jesus as a boy, or a young man, watching Joseph at work, asking questions in the inquisitive way of children, picking up the same piece of wood and running his fingers down it. Jesus must have known much about wood, having grown up around it from an early age. Imagine him looking at the grain in the wood and estimating the age of the tree it came from.

Now pick up your nail and touch it. Feel the sharpness of its tip with your finger. Imagine Joseph warning Jesus to be careful, as he must have done now and again, when Jesus went near the nails, the saw or some particularly splintered piece of wood.

Then think of another piece of wood, larger than this one and far more deadly: a cross. Imagine you are touching that cross now.

Did Jesus ever have an inkling, as Joseph hammered in the workshop, that one day soldiers would hammer nails into him? Yet when that time came, Jesus was not thinking of himself; he was thinking of those soldiers, pleading to God to forgive them because they didn't know what they were doing.

Pause for a while now, and let Jesus speak to you, as you meditate on the wood, about forgiveness and about his love for you.

Then, when you are ready, use the nail to hammer the two pieces of wood together into a cross. What does doing this action teach you?

When you have done this, pause for a little while to pray, holding your cross. You can take your cross home with you after the service if you wish.

50 Jigsaw

UP TO 60

This method of prayer can be used with a small or a large group of people of virtually any age. If your congregation is large just remember to get a jigsaw with a lot of pieces! We first did this prayer ritual in connection with the parable of the talents when we were thinking about what gifts we had and how they related to other's gifts.

Resources
You will need: a jigsaw with about the same number of pieces as the size of the congregation plus a few spare pieces; a basket; pens; one person at the front who knows the jigsaw well enough to help assemble it.

Think carefully about the picture on the jigsaw. You might want to use a picture of a church, a 3D jigsaw of a church, or a picture of Christ (some old master paintings are available on jigsaw) or maybe you might like to make your own by mounting a large colour print or photocopy on card with spray mounting glue (this is less likely to make the picture wrinkle than ordinary glue). You could then cut it out using a craft knife or scissors.

Method
Put the jigsaw pieces in a basket and pass them around the church. Also pass the pens around at the same time. Invite each person to take a jigsaw piece and a pen. Then read the following script.

The jigsaw script
You each have a jigsaw piece. Look at it now. We have each been given special gifts and talents that we can use to help others, a bit like the lugs on your jigsaw piece. Ask God now about the talents you have. Thank him for them. (Pause)

Now think about where this jigsaw piece fits into the bigger picture. Ask God to show you the best ways to use those talents. (Long pause)

Now think about the other pieces of the jigsaw and the people who have interacted with you and helped you. Thank God for their gifts and pray for them for a while now. (Long pause)

Now write your name on your jigsaw piece and come and place it at the front of the church. (Pause until everyone has placed their pieces at the front, aided by a helper.) *We can see that there are pieces missing from the jigsaw. So let's pray for the people who are missing this morning because they are ill* (pause), *people who are too busy or stressed to come* (pause), *people who have left us or who have lost their faith* (pause), *and the people we know who we would love to come and join us but for one reason or another aren't ready to yet.* (Pause) *If you wish to, come and write the name of one, or several of these people on a piece and add it to the picture now. Lord Jesus, come and touch these people wherever they may be.*

Finally allow others to come and view the completed picture.

51 Stones

Stones are rich in symbolism and are often mentioned in the Bible. For this reason they can be a useful resource for meditations or prayer rituals. Here is just one stones meditation, based on 1 Peter 2.

Resources:
You will need: a collection of lots of different stones, perhaps from a nearby beach (enough stones so that each person can have one each with some spare besides); a bowlful of water; a waterproof mat or tray to build a cairn on.

Method
Arrange the stones at the front of the church so that they can easily be seen. If your building allows this, gather the people around the stones in a circle. Then appoint a good reader to read the following script.

The stones script
Focus your eyes on this pile of stones for a moment. Look carefully at them. Look at all their slightly different shapes and colours, their imperfections and their beauty. Some stones may have little cracks in, where dirt has been trapped. Maybe you feel like that at the moment. When the grime of modern society seems to get to you, or you feel guilty inside. (Short pause)

Some of the stones may have tiny pieces of glittery quartz embedded in them. Maybe these remind you of exciting times, or the day when you discovered you had a new talent. (Short pause)

Some of the stones are hard granite or flint, others are made of softer rock. Do you feel soft and vulnerable? Or have you hardened yourself so you can't be hurt. (Short pause)

Some of these stones are smooth and even in shape, having been worn away by their experiences in the sea. (Short pause)

Others are uneven, having been chipped or injured recently by another stone. (Short pause)

When you are ready, come up to the pile, and choose a stone that reminds you a little of yourself and look at it closely for a few minutes. (Pause for a few moments and allow people to come up and choose a stone. Give them time to sit and look at their stone for a while.)

St Peter called Jesus the Living Stone: rejected by human beings; smashed and thrown away, but chosen by God and precious to him; more precious than diamonds or rubies. (Pause)

Peter said we too are like living stones. We may feel cracked or tired. We may feel that we don't fit or are too hurt to want to connect with anyone. Yet we're being built into a spiritual temple: polished and smoothed and beautified and made into a building for God to live in. Look at your stone again, and think about the things you want God to change in you to make you a more beautiful person. (Pause)

Then, when you are ready, and if you feel comfortable about it, dunk your stone in the bowl of water till it is wet all over and make a cairn with the other wet stones. As you dunk the stone, offer yourself to God once more. Then, as you build the cairn, watch how the water has transformed the stone, making it shine with a new beauty. (Pause)

'You are the chosen race, the King's priests, the holy nation, God's own people, chosen to proclaim the wonderful acts of God, who called you out of darkness into his own marvellous light' (1 Peter 2:9 GNB).

You may find that some people might wish to take their stones home with them after the ritual is over, so it is good to make allowances for this.

ANY NUMBER

52 Reminders

This is a way of bringing our prayers from inside the church into the outside world, and also a good way of reminding us about important things. There are a number of variations on this prayer idea. I first came across it when an Orthodox priest told me that he always carried a nail around on Good Friday as a reminder of Christ's sufferings for us.

Resources
The resources depend on which variation you decide to use.
You will need: either a bag of nails (small enough to easily fit into a pocket and large enough to not be easily lost or dropped where a child or animal may be hurt by them) or a bag of small stones (again a good size for a pocket) or a packet of mixed nuts in their shells.

Method for version 1 (nails)
Put the nails into a suitable container or bowl and pass them around the congregation until each person has one nail. You might then wish to have a Bible reading, dramatic piece or poem about the crucifixion. When you have finished, ask everyone to keep their nail with them throughout the day and whenever they touch it to remember what Christ did for us and to thank him.

Method for version 2 (stones)
Read the Bible passage about Jacob's dream (Genesis 28:10–15). Then appoint a good reader to read the following script.

Jacob's dream script
Look at your stone now. Jacob rested his head on a stone. He used it as a pillow. It was a lot larger than your stone, but just as hard and perhaps made of the same rock, and as Jacob slept God gave him a dream about his future. He told him he would never desert him, he gave him a promise that Jacob would have the land on which he was lying, and that he would have many descendants.

Now, as you hold your stone, pray that God will guide you and show you the way to go in the future. (Short pause) Think firstly about the little daily decisions we all need to make. Pray that we make the right ones. (Pause) Then think about the big decisions. Perhaps your future plans all seem fairly clear, or maybe you're not so sure, but God is concerned

about all our lives. Pray now for the bigger decisions, or for people you know who have to make big decisions. (Pause)

Trust that God will show us what is right, whether it be in dreams, visions, or the more mundane coincidences or opportunities that seem to fall in our laps. Now put your stone in your pocket and keep it there for a few days, and when you touch your stone remember what God said to Jacob: 'I will watch over you wherever you go, and I will bring you back to this land. I will not leave you until I have done what I have promised you.'
(Genesis 28:15)

Perhaps you might also like to leave your stone under your pillow when you go to bed, and pray that, like Jacob, God will guide you through your dreams too.

Method for version 3 (mixed nuts)
In the autumn it is possible to buy bags of mixed nuts in their shells, for example walnuts, pecan nuts, hazelnuts and almonds. This might be a good season in which to spend a session praying for the different types of outreach projects happening in your church or your town. (Remember to check that no one has an allergy to nuts!)

Place the nuts at the front or in the centre of the church, in a place where many people can see them and place the different kinds of nuts on different pieces of card labelled with the different projects going on in the church. Then read the parable of the sower (Matthew 13:1–9, 18–23). Mention that the nuts represent the many different sorts of seed being sown in our church or town today – the different outreach projects suiting different people's needs and personalities. Then invite people to come to the front and take a nut from one of the piles and put it in their pocket. Invite people during the week when they find the nut in their pocket, to remember to pray for that particular project, that this seed would grow and produce good fruit.

Other variations
You can do a version of this as an intercessory prayer if you have a situation you are really worried about, or someone you

wish to pray for as a church. You could give out small cards to carry around, pictures, or little pieces of cloth with knots in (like knotted handkerchiefs) to remind everyone, whenever they find the item in their pocket, to pray for the situation.

UP TO 60/ADAPTABLE

53 Prisoners

This prayer idea can be used any time you are praying for those in prison. It is particularly suitable for those times when you wish to pray for those who are imprisoned because of their beliefs, especially their Christian beliefs.

Resources
You will need: information about those in prison (this can be obtained from *Amnesty International* or, if you are specifically praying for suffering Christians, you can get information from organisations such as *Open Doors*. The Internet is another good source of this sort of information.); a large fat candle with barbed wire wrapped around it; a circle of chains (these could either be small, black paper chains, or real chains with weak links composed of twist ties).

Method
Place the candle in the centre of the prayer group and, if the group isn't too big, place the circle of chains around the whole group. Otherwise place the chains in a circle around the candle.

Then read some stories from the *Amnesty International* or *Open Doors* information about those in prison because of their beliefs. You might decide to have several people give short accounts of specific people's problems, or you might wish to concentrate on the political problems or problems of being a Christian in different countries.

Then pass the candle around the group (making sure that the barbed wire is towards the top of the candle so that people don't cut themselves on it). As people get the candle ask them to pray for those in prison, aloud or silently as they wish. They may just wish to

say a person's name or the name of the church in a country, for example 'Christians in China'.

When everyone has had a chance to hold the candle, place it back in the middle of the circle and invite everyone to gather around and break the circle of chains. As you do this you may wish to make a pronouncement of some sort such as:

'The Spirit of the Lord is on me because he has anointed me to preach good news to the poor. He has sent me to proclaim freedom for the prisoners…' (Luke 4:18/Isaiah 61:1,2).

Alternatively, you could sing or play a song about freedom, such as 'Freedom is coming', while the chains are being broken.

UP TO 60

54 Ascension

These prayer ideas were written for Ascension Sunday. To start the service we went outside to read from Acts chapter one (when Jesus was taken up into heaven) and a single helium balloon was released so that we could watch it disappear into the sky and have some sense of what the apostles might have been feeling. Then we went inside for the rest of the service which had included the following prayer ritual.

Resources
You will need: a large pile of slightly wet sand (play sand is best but sharp sand will do); a plastic sheet to place under the sand if there is carpet that may be damaged; a fence of some sort (we used a puppy play pen which was like a small iron fence, but you may have access to police tape or something else appropriate); nightlight candles; some instrumental dance music with a strong drum rhythm (or you could use a classical piece of music with a driving rhythm).

Method
Find a central spot in the church big enough to be surrounded by people. Place the groundsheet (if needed) on the ground and make a pile of sand on it. Flatten the sand to

make a small flat 'hilltop' and then get someone to take off their shoes and make two clear footprints upon the sand. Surround this with the fence for most of the service, then when the prayer ritual is due to begin remove the fence. It may be helpful for you to mention that the sand and footprints are symbolic of the hill that Jesus ascended from. In Israel there is a hill with dents in the rock and legend says that this is the hill from where Jesus ascended. We don't know whether that is true or not, but the footprints are a powerful symbol.

It might also be good to mention that Jesus ascended so that he could be with us all through the Holy Spirit, wherever we are, and that the following litany is particularly inviting him to come now and help some of the situations of suffering in the world.

Invite people to come and surround the footprints, to sit, kneel or stand by them, and to light a candle for some situation that you really want Jesus to come and help. Then get a good leader, reader or priest to read the first line of the following litany. Invite everyone to join in the response, which for every line is 'Come Lord Jesus'. As the litany starts, play the music with the driving rhythm and ask the leader to pray this litany with a lot of emphasis, perhaps even almost shouting. If you go through the litany twice, you will find people will get more 'into' the prayer as it progresses.

Please add current news or political situations to the litany to personalise it. This works particularly well if you can add a justice situation you feel passionately about so that there is an energy and emphasis in your prayers.

To all hungry people,
Come, Lord Jesus.
Where children are dying,
Come, Lord Jesus.
Where widows are mourning,
Come, Lord Jesus.
To victims of violence,
Come, Lord Jesus.
To those suffering bombing,
Come, Lord Jesus.
And those caught in conflict,
Come, Lord Jesus.

To all refugees,
Come, Lord Jesus.
To those who are homeless,
Come, Lord Jesus.
To those who feel hopeless,
Come, Lord Jesus.
To those suicidal,
Come, Lord Jesus.

And those who feel trapped,
Come, Lord Jesus.
Give wisdom to Parliament,
Come, Lord Jesus.
To stop all injustice,
Come, Lord Jesus.
To those slowly dying,
Come, Lord Jesus.
And all those in mourning,
Come, Lord Jesus.
To those who've been tortured,
Come, Lord Jesus.
The unfairly imprisoned,
Come, Lord Jesus.
Those suffering in silence,
Come, Lord Jesus.
To all those forgotten,
Come, Lord Jesus.
Come, Lord Jesus.
Amen.

55 Let your lights shine

`UP TO 60/ADAPTABLE`

We used this prayer ritual during an Advent service. It could also be used as part of a service based on the Sermon on the Mount or even Romans chapter 7. It may not be suitable for safety reasons where young children are involved.

Resources
You will need: a set of Christmas tree lights (the white ones look best). Try and get those lights that only work when all the bulbs are in place. Check that all the bulbs are OK before doing this and that the electric lights are safe.

Method
Remove all the tree lights from the wire and unplug (for safety!). Give a lightbulb to each person and ask them to pray about the situations they have found most difficult lately.

Perhaps they are feeling useless, or finding it hard to make a decision of conscience. Perhaps they might feel they aren't living a very good Christian life or are finding that, despite themselves, they keep doing the wrong thing. Then ask each person to come and put a light in a holder, as a sign that they want to give themselves to God once more and ask for the power of the Holy Spirit to come and help them in their difficult situation. If people wish, they can pray instead for a friend who is going through a difficult time.

When all the lightbulbs are in place, then switch on the power. Nothing may happen. If the lights don't come on, mention that this is because every bulb is important to make the treelights work, just as each one of us is important to God even if we think we're useless. Switch off the power and get some volunteers to help you ensure all the bulbs are correctly fitted, then switch on once more. Hopefully the lights will then shine! You may wish to place these lights around something: a Christmas tree, a cross, a road sign or some other symbolic object. You may also find it helpful to read the following quote written by St John Chrysostom, if it is applicable:

'Don't tell me "it is impossible for me to influence others." If you are a Christian, it is impossible for you *not* to influence others! ... So, do not offend God. If you say, "the sun cannot shine," you offend Him. If you say, "I, a Christian cannot be of service to others," you have offended Him and called Him a liar. It is easier for the sun not to shine than for a Christian not to do so ... If we arrange our affairs in an orderly manner, these things will certainly follow quite naturally. It is impossible for a Christian's light to lie concealed. So brilliant a lamp cannot be hidden.'

(Taken from Homily no. 20 on the Acts of the Apostles.)

`UP TO 60/ADAPTABLE`

56 The Valley of Dry Bones

We used this method of prayer at a service when the theme was Ezekiel 37 and the Valley of Dry Bones. It is more of an

intercession really, for our friends and other people we know.

Resources
You will need: a large picture or photocopy of a skeleton; marker pens; a stand or board of some sort so people can see more easily (optional).

Method
Explain that we are going to have a time of intercession for those people we might know who are feeling dead or dry or broken for some reason. Invite each person to come up and write a name on one of the bones of the skeleton, or even some initials if they wish the situation to be fairly private. After all the names have been placed on the bones, pray a concluding prayer that God would come and help these people to live once more.

 57 The wall ANY NUMBER

This prayer method is good for an alternative confession time when people can focus, not only on the things they have done wrong, but also on other things that are getting in the way of them worshipping God.

Resources
You will need: a stack of large cardboard boxes (enough to build a wall); pens or pencils and sheets of paper; marker pens; tape to stick the box lids down; some sort of symbol (a lamp or Communion table perhaps); some volunteers to help; a cross, small enough to be hand-held.

Method
Take the boxes and on the side of each of them write labels such as 'stresses', 'worries', 'sins', 'lack of time', 'illness', 'guilt', 'cynicism', 'pain', 'disappointment', 'apathy', 'fear'. Have the boxes distributed around the building so that there is a box near each member of the congregation. Explain that we are going to have a few minutes of quiet when we think about those things that get in the way of us worshipping God: perhaps worries about everyday life, job worries, money worries or something that has become

very stressful for them. Then ask people to write all the things that come to mind on a piece of paper and fold it tightly so that the writing cannot be seen. Say that these papers will remain private and be destroyed after the service. Then ask people to place each piece of paper in the nearest box and seal it with a short strip of tape. Depending on the size of the congregation either ask everyone to bring a box to the front, or just a number of volunteers to bring up the boxes from the congregation. Have a volunteer handy at the front to help build the wall. Build it in front of some sort of symbol for God such as a lamp, a Trinity symbol, or the Communion table if you are going to have Communion later. (The cross would probably be an inappropriate symbol on this occasion.) Make sure that as much as possible, the wall hides the symbol so it cannot be seen. Then pray the following prayer together or use an appropriate confession prayer.

Lord God,
We want to meet you,
But so many things get in our way.
We sometimes feel so guilty,
For the things we've done wrong.
We are so sorry.
Sometimes we're even guilty,
When we did the right thing,
But someone ended up hurt.
We sometimes feel so crushed,
By stresses, worries, and pain.
They feel like a brick wall between us and you,
And we find it hard to meet you.
Forgive us the things we've done wrong.
Heal us and calm our fears.
Jesus reach out and break the walls down,
Come and meet us now.
And show us how to pray once more.
Amen.

When the prayer is finished, pray an appropriate absolution prayer (such as the one below) and while it is being said get a volunteer (perhaps holding or wearing a cross) to kick the wall down. If this prayer ritual is performed at the beginning of a Communion service, you may wish to keep the boxes lying scattered around to remind people as they come up for Communion (clear a path through the aisles though so nobody trips over the boxes).

God has forgiven you,
Christ has come to meet you,
He's broken down our walls of guilt,
By the power of the cross.
Come and meet him now.

ANY NUMBER

58 A time capsule

This is a chance, not only to pray intercessory prayer in a creative way but also, some time later, to have a time of thanksgiving prayer.

Resources
You will need: some good quality paper and pens (preferably ones which have ink which will not run); a time capsule or airtight container (some shops now sell dedicated time capsules); some volunteers to help when the capsule is dug up; OHP (optional).

Method
Explain that you are going to have a time of intercessory prayer when you write prayers for events that are happening in the church and in the world at that time. Tell the congregation that these written prayers are going to be buried in a time capsule and dug up at a later date for a time of thanksgiving. Therefore, the subjects of the prayers (unlike the writing letters to God exercise) should be public rather than private. Don't forget to tell the congregation how long you are planning to leave the prayers buried for. One year might be an appropriate length of time to do this for.

You may wish to suggest some subjects for these prayers, or invite members of the congregation to suggest subjects, perhaps putting these titles on the overhead projector. Then pens and paper should be handed around so that people can write their intercessions. It is also a good idea to remind people to write neatly so that they can be read at a later date. When people have finished writing their prayers ask them to come up to the front of the church and place their prayers into the capsule. You may wish to wait until the end of the service to bury the capsule, but, whenever you decide to do it, allow the congregation to surround the capsule and witness it being buried. As you bury the capsule you might wish to pray some sort of 'Lord hear our prayers' prayer that completes the exercise.

A few weeks before the digging up of the prayer time capsule, advertise in the notice sheet and on the church notice boards the fact that it is going to be dug up, so that the people who wrote the prayers are reminded of the event. Dig up the prayer time capsule at the start of the service and have some volunteers who knew what the original prayer subjects were to look through the prayers while the rest of the service is going on. Then have a time, near the end of the service, when the volunteers can give some updates on some of the subjects mentioned. Follow this with a time of thanksgiving for all the prayers that have been answered and a following time of intercession for situations that are continuing to be difficult.

Instead of having the volunteers looking through the prayers during the service, you may decide to dig up the capsule one week and have the follow-up and thanksgiving session the next week. You may also wish to display some of the prayers at the back of the church, if the people that wrote them have no objections to this being done.

ANY NUMBER

59 Slavery

This meditation gives us a chance to think about the slaves in Egypt and compare them to people today who work very hard and suffer from the burden of debt.

Resources
You will need: coffee beans (any type will do but obviously fairly-traded might be a good idea). You may also decide to compare this meditation with some sort of practical method of helping others, such as a sale of fairly-traded goods or a justice campaign of some sort. Instead of coffee beans you may decide to use some bitter herbs or parsley in salt water. It would be better to use herbs if there are young children present due to the dangers of choking and they may be upset at being left out.

Method

Appoint a good reader to read a passage about the plight of the Hebrew slaves in Egypt (such as Exodus 5:1–21). Then give out the coffee beans or herbs and ask the congregation to eat them. Say some words such as the following script while people are eating.

The coffee script

We have heard the plight of the Israelites in Egypt. And we think that for us slavery has been abolished. But many still suffer the conditions of a slave, trapped in a sweatshop factory in countries such as China or Taiwan. They are unable to complain for fear of being arrested, or so trapped by debt that they cannot earn a proper living, like those who grow coffee and tea who are at the mercy of the large corporations who buy their beans. In some countries there are still children who have to work in miserable conditions and who never have the chance to play. Let's spend a few minutes in silence praying for them now.

Finish with the following litany or something similar to it. Remember to update the litany according to any new news information about people being treated badly that comes to light.

We remember the plight of the Jews enslaved in Egypt,
We taste the bitterness of their slavery.
We pray for those working in clothes factory sweatshops,
We taste the bitterness of their slavery.
We pray for those who are starving because of their nation's debts,
We taste the bitterness of their slavery.
We pray for coffee farmers who can hardly scrape a living,
We taste the bitterness of their slavery.
We pray for those who work in dangerous conditions,
We taste the bitterness of their slavery.
We pray for those children who have never had a childhood,
We taste the bitterness of their slavery.
We pray for the sex-slaves who can't see an escape,
We taste the bitterness of their slavery.

We pray for those crushed by human rights abuses,
We taste the bitterness of their slavery.
We pray for those trapped inside caring for the sick,
We taste the bitterness of their slavery.
We pray for those on drugs who don't know how to quit,
We taste the bitterness of their slavery.
We pray for all who suffer violence and oppression,
We taste the bitterness of their slavery.

Set them all free, my God,
Show us how to break their chains.
Bring them to your promised land of freedom.

60 Loving hands

This prayer ritual is a way of making a resolution to serve God and to serve others better. It could be combined with an appropriate service of commitment to God (such as a baptism, confirmation or anniversary of the dedication of the church).

Resources

You will need: body paint or make up. Body drawing pens are also available nowadays. In some special cases you may even decide to use henna paste (but it may be best to keep the design small and discreet in that case – henna designs can sometimes last weeks before they wear off, although when they are scrubbed regularly they may last much less time than that).

Method

Prepare the paint or make-up first and have it ready at the front of the church. Then get a good reader to read the script below. Instead of appointing a reader you may decide to give the words to everyone to say. Invite people who wish to participate in the ritual to come up to the front of the church, perhaps forming two queues, if that is the way the church is used to taking Communion. The act of going to the front of the church can become part of the act of commitment. Have two volunteers at the front of the two queues to draw a heart on the palms of the hands of the

person behind them, then invite that person to do the same with the person behind them. An alternative method, if the group is small, is to have more paint available and allow the group to split into twos to spend a longer time drawing the hearts on each other's palms. Be aware though that some people may not feel ready to participate in such a commitment.

The loving hands script
Jesus said 'Now I give you a new commandment: love one another. As I have loved you so you must love one another. If you have love for one another, then everyone will know that you are my disciples.' (John 13:34,35 GNB)

Lord Jesus, our hands are empty without you. We are bankrupt of love and often crippled by bitterness. We do not know how to love you or each other properly. But now we give our empty hands to you. We want to learn to love, and to spread that love in a love-starved world. We give ourselves to you, as a new beginning. As we write on our palms, write your script of love into our lives. And as we draw these hearts on our hands, fill those hands with your love and strength, to be your love in action. Amen.

61 Burdens

UP TO 60

This prayer ritual was designed to help us focus on the burdens that we are carrying, and to encourage us to pray about them and give them to God. We found that actually carrying real burdens helped us think more carefully about the problems we were carrying around inside. It was also wonderful to actually have the refreshment of drinking real water during the service.

Resources
You will need: bricks, large stones or packages of some sort (enough for each congregation member); a large cross; jars of water and glasses. (Make sure there is enough water for everyone to have a drink if they wish. You may also wish to chill the water to make it more refreshing.)

Space must be cleared in the church for the people to process up to the front of the building, or around the building if it is a small one. You will also need a volunteer (or several volunteers) to give out the water.

Method
At the beginning of the service make sure that the bricks or stones are placed so that there is one near every chair or pew. Then appoint a good reader to read the following script.

The burdens script
Jesus said, 'Come to me, all you who are tired from carrying heavy loads, and I will give you rest. Take my yoke and put it on you, and learn from me, because I am gentle and humble in spirit; and you will find rest. For the yoke I will give you is easy, and the load I will put on you is light'. (Matthew 11:28–30 GNB)

Pick up your brick or stone now and think about what burdens you are carrying at the moment. They might be big burdens or they might be relatively small ones. (Pause)

Now ask God if there are any burdens you are carrying that you didn't realise were there: things that are weighing you down. Talk to God about these for a while. (Pause)

Now think for a while about your friends. Are there any who have a particularly heavy load to bear at the moment? Pray for them now. (Pause)

When you are ready, come to the front of the building and place your stone at the foot of the cross. Then come and take a glass of water. As you drink, pray that Jesus refreshes you and your troubled friends with his living water for he said, 'All those who drink this water will be thirsty again. But all those who drink the water that I will give them will never be thirsty again. The water that I will give will become a spring welling up to eternal life.' (author's paraphrase of John 4:13,14)

62 Perfume

This prayer can be used in conjunction with a number of different Bible passages. It can be a very moving and healing experience to have someone anoint you with perfume, and of course the smell lingers for a while after the experience is over, reminding you of it.

Resources
You will need: some bottles of perfumed oil. (The best kind to use would actually be aromatherapy massage oil which can be bought from most chemists these days. This will be fine with most people's skin and shouldn't cause any adverse allergic reactions.) Enhance the oil with the scent of your choice, but avoid flower perfumes or really strong scents that might cause allergic reactions or be too pungent and unpleasant. Check that whatever perfume you use is safe to use on skin.

Method
Read an appropriate Bible passage such as John 12:1–8 (when Mary anoints Jesus with perfume), then explain that we are going to have a time when we anoint each other by placing a small drop of perfumed oil on each of the other person's hands. The best method of actually organising the anointing depends on the size of the congregation. Put the perfumed oil in suitable containers to make it easy to obtain the oil without undue shaking or squeezing of bottles. (It is best not to use plastic containers for this as some plastics may absorb the smell.)

In smaller groups, it may be better to have everyone doing the anointing and everyone being anointed. This emphasises the servanthood aspect of this prayer ritual. This can be organised in small congregations by having people split into pairs to anoint the person next to them. As an alternative, in larger groups you could have a queue and the person at the front of the queue anoints the next person in it. Each person is then anointed by the person in front of them and anoints the person behind them.

Some congregations may be uncomfortable with this method, and also if the size of congregation is very large you may wish to have a few volunteers at the front of the church to do the anointing.

You may wish to leave the ritual silent and open for people to interpret themselves, or you may wish to have some, or all, of the following words spoken or projected at the front of the church.

As Mary perfumed Jesus to show him her love,
So I perfume you to share his love.
As Samuel anointed David to be a king,
So I anoint you to rule as a servant.
As Moses anointed Aaron to be a priest of God,
So I anoint you to show others the way to God.

63 Soil

This prayer ritual is designed to be used during a time of confession. Sometimes it can be useful to have concrete symbols such as earth and water at these times, to help us think about how the bad attitudes of society rub off on us.

Resources
You will need: bowls of earth (or compost or mud); bowls of water (you may decide to convert a large bowl of water into a fountain using one of the small fountain pumps available at garden centres); towels; OHP (optional).

Method
Explain that we are going to have a time of confession and that we are going to use some earth to help us in it. Pass the bowls of earth around the congregation and ask them to dip the palms of their hands in the earth as it goes around. Meanwhile, pray a prayer such as the one below, or have it projected on the wall so that the whole congregation can join in with it.

Lord,
You said we should be in the world,
but not be part of it.
Yet when we live so closely,
Deep inside a culture
That never thinks of you,
Their values dirty us,
And suddenly we feel cheap.
When our friends fuel gossip
And we say nothing,
When our neighbours fuel injustice
And we do nothing,
When our community
Behaves badly
And we go along with them.
Because being different is hard,
Forgive us, Lord.
Wash our dirty hands clean.
And give us the courage
To do the right thing.
Amen.

Then when everyone has had a chance to touch the soil, invite people to come up to the fountain or water bowl and wash their hands. You may like to pray some sort of absolution prayer as this is done, or perhaps read the following Bible passage.

'At that time a fountain will be opened to the people of Israel and Jerusalem, a fountain to cleanse them of all their sins and uncleanness. And the Lord of Heaven's army declares "In that day I will get rid of every vestige of idol worship…"' (Zechariah 13:1,2a *Living Bible*).

UP TO 60/ADAPTABLE

64 Letting go

This prayer ritual is appropriate to do at any time where things may be changing and something or someone has to go. Perhaps someone is moving away from the church, or perhaps the structure of the service is changing in some way. You may even decide that a variation on this ritual may be appropriate for a funeral or memorial service, but please be very careful to find out the wishes and the feelings of others in this case. Only use it if others find it helpful and healing.

Resources
You will need: a large cross; a collection of fallen leaves. Try and collect some that are as beautiful and colourful as possible. (You may decide to save some for this purpose, or you may decide that this ritual is best done in the autumn.)

Method
Give a leaf to each person in the group and allow them to sit looking at it for a while. Then appoint a good reader to read the following script.

The letting go script
God is never static. He is always leading us to new places on our journey to heaven and sometimes that means letting go of people, places and things that are familiar to us. These leaves have let go, and they are more beautiful for doing so.

And now they have gone, the tree has room to grow new branches when the warmth of the sun hits it anew in the spring.

Abraham had to let go of his town and move to a land full of promises. The Jews had to leave the familiarity of Egypt on a journey through the desert. The apostles had to give up their fishing nets to follow Christ. And Jesus had to give up life itself for us.

Think now about… (the thing or the person you are letting go of. Alternatively, you may wish to make this more general about smaller changes in people's lives.) Think about all the good things he/she/it gave you and thank God for them. (Pause)

Now focus on one thing – a particularly good thing that this person/thing gave you and thank God for it now. (Pause)

Now ask God to show you a new thing that he wishes to grow in you when the warmth of his love hits you like the spring sun hits the trees. Perhaps God might not show you this thing straightaway, but pray that it comes soon. (Pause)

Then, when you are ready, and if you feel that you can, come and let go of your leaf at

the foot of the cross as a sign that you are letting go of the past and moving on. Not forgetting, not saying that the past was bad, but just saying goodbye and giving it to God. (If you do decide to use this at a funeral you may wish to place the leaves on the coffin and bury or burn them too if appropriate).

Jesus said, 'I assure you that anyone who leaves home or wife or brothers or parents or children for the sake of the kingdom of God will receive much more in the present age and eternal life in the age to come.' (Luke 18:29,30 GNB)

Visions

The journey of an alternative worship community

Our community in York started back in 1989 when a group of people met together to plan a Christian arts and music nightclub that would be using a disused warehouse for a month as part of the events surrounding a mission in York Minster. The group, which was then known as *Warehouse* was born. Many people from different churches were involved in this event.

However, when the excitement of the initial project was over, a smaller group of us continued to meet together. Our aim was to explore community, the arts, and mission within a post-modern culture. We wanted, eventually, to have a venue similar to the original *Warehouse*, to be a Christian arts and music venue, but we also wanted to be able to start a late night multimedia service, similar to the events that were happening in Sheffield at that time. We attached ourselves, for pastoral support, to the church of St Michael-le-Belfrey, which had been famous in the 1970s for pioneering new and exciting ways of utilising art, music and drama within worship. Graham Cray, our vicar at the time, was particularly helpful and supportive, encouraging us in our efforts to find artistic ways of expressing our worship that would be appropriate to the young adult subcultures within York.

In August 1991 we had the first *Warehouse* Anglican multimedia church service. It was initially an experiment, to which we invited many older and wiser people than ourselves (including the Bishop of Selby), to give comments, help and advice. We then officially opened our church doors to the public in March 1992.

Our initial service was a dance-based teaching service, with half an hour of sung worship, which was performed over dance tracks we had written ourselves. This was followed by a time of teaching, which was little different to a standard church sermon. This service happened once a month. Over time, we gradually realised that this approach wasn't very effective within a culture that is so visual and experiential in nature. We experimented, becoming more visual in our teaching – using video and word loops as part of a service which became more integrated in its approach to the subject being approached, whilst still being relevant to dance music and club culture. We have often been invited to produce artwork, slides and video for secular club nights in the York area, and more recently we have become involved in a project to launch a Christian multimedia ambient café venue in York. The rise of late night café culture in the last couple of years has particularly interested us; the intimacy of a café venue lends itself to deep conversations in a way that nightclubs do not.

A couple of years after we began our dance service, we started our Communion service. The Communion now takes place on the first Sunday of the month and the dance service on the third Sunday of the month. The Communion was more meditative in style, using gentle ambient synthesizer music throughout. This was where we began our first experiments in integrating more experimental and practical forms of prayer. We soon discovered just how powerful these were, both as a way of communicating with God and as a way of discovering more about ourselves. We were inspired by other groups doing similar things with their worship throughout the country and integrated some of their ideas into our worship. We also changed our name from *Warehouse* to *Visions,* to reflect our multimedia nature and also our desire to have dreams and visions about the shape of the church of the future.

Nowadays, *Visions* meet together on three Sundays a month. As well as the dance and Communion services, on the second Sunday of the month we meet for prayer and use a medieval labyrinth, candles, plainchant music and Bibles to aid us in our prayer. We also have a midweek small group where we meet to explore and discuss our faith together.

We are just one of the many experimental services that have sprung up around the country in recent years. Stylistically these alternative worship services are very varied, yet one thing all these new congregations seem to have in common is a desire for worship to become more participatory. They are inspiring others to become less like consumers and to take a more active part in the planning and execution of their worship meetings. For art as part of worship is not an elitist thing. It is a tool we can all use to enrich our prayer lives and enhance our devotions, enabling us to express our love for God in new ways.

www.visions-york.org

Index of types of prayer

Index of the Church year

(including Liturgical Feasts and Christian themes)

Index of Bible Passages

These Bible readings are either mentioned in the following prayer ideas or would be an appropriate reading to use in conjunction with them. Many of the readings for the intercessory prayer ideas are interchangeable (see Index 2).

Index for different congregation sizes

Some of these prayer ideas can be used with any size of group, even large churches with hundreds of peple in the congregation. Others work better in a small group setting, where everyone is able to share information with one another. Many of the prayer ideas work best with a medium-sized group of people, about the size of a parish church congregation. It is wise not to be too strict in your interpretation of these guidelines, as congregations and buildings differ so much.

ANY NUMBER

Ideas that will work with any size of group.

UP TO 60/ADAPTABLE

Ideas that work best with a medium-sized group of people but can be adapted to suit larger sizes by having more resources available (eg 5 globes to pass round the congregation instead of one, or more than one "station" where handwashing can take place).

UP TO 60

Ideas that work best with a medium sized group of people (up to around 60)

page no

UNDER 20

Ideas that work best with a small group of people (up to about 20)